INTRODUCTION

What is economics? Even if you do not have a clear definition of economics in mind, you probably have some good ideas regarding what economics is all about. On a personal level, you know that economics involves jobs and income and whether you can afford to buy things that you want. If you are running a business or plan to do so, economics involves concerns such as costs, revenues, profits, and how to start or expand your business. On a national level, economics looks at issues such as the overall levels of prices, unemployment, and economic growth. Economics also involves international issues such as trade and exchange rates. Some people are under the impression that economics is only about the study of money. Economists do study money, but economics includes much more than this.

The basic economic problem is scarcity. Scarcity exists because economic resources are limited, but people's wants are not. Because of scarcity, we cannot have all of the goods and services that we would like for ourselves and for others, and therefore we have to make choices. Economics is very much about making choices and deciding how to make the best use of scarce resources. With this in mind, we can define economics as a social science concerned with the way society chooses to use its scarce resources to produce goods and services to satisfy people's wants.

The five volumes in our series *Student Handbook to Economics* provide a solid foundation for learning about major topics related to economics and for learning about different approaches to studying economics. *Microeconomics* looks at economics from the viewpoint of individuals, businesses, or industries. It involves studying about supply and demand, or how prices are established in a market economic system. What role the government should play when markets do not work perfectly is another important microeconomic topic.

1

Macroeconomics looks at economics from the perspective of the whole economy. Macroeconomics addresses problems such as inflation, unemployment, and why the economy has its ups and downs. Macroeconomics also addresses what the government and central bank can try to do about problems in the economy. Our *International Economics* volume investigates topics such as globalization, economic development, trade and trade barriers, exchange rates, and different types of economic systems.

The fourth volume in our economics series, *History of Economic Thought*, takes a historical perspective and traces economic philosophy from Aristotle to the present, addressing the interesting and important topic of the philosophies underlying various economic theories. The fifth volume in our series, *Entrepreneurship*, focuses on the innovative business side of economics. What are the types of business organizations? What is the role of market research? How can you create a company or expand a company? Each of the five volumes provides a framework for better understanding economic topics and issues.

Why is it important to study economics? It is important because it will help you to make better decisions on a personal level. With a better understanding of the world around you, you will be able to make better choices as a consumer and producer or entrepreneur. You will have a better understanding of local, national, and international events and trends covered by the media. You will become a more informed participant in our democracy, and a more informed participant in our global economy. We wish you the best as you embark on your exciting adventure.

CHAPTER 1

THE BIG PICTURE

The business of America is business.
—Calvin Coolidge

Getting and spending, we lay waste our powers . . .
—William Wordsworth

I perceive clearly that the extreme business energy and that almost maniacal Appetite for wealth prevalent in the United States, are parts of amelioration and progress.
—Walt Whitman

Complex issues are sometimes easier to understand through examples or analogies, and thus a good way to understand the role of business in our economy is to begin in a surprising place—in this case, ABC's live-action series *Lost*. One of the most popular shows on television, *Lost* was critically acclaimed. It received many awards—including the Emmy and Golden Globe—and achieved almost cult status among fans. To what can we ascribe *Lost*'s popularity? Setting aside the flashbacks and polar bears and endless debate about what it all actually meant, the show was built upon a simple but compelling premise: An airplane crashes on a mysterious island. Left with nothing but a few tools and articles of clothing from the airplane, the survivors must work together to find food and shelter. How will they manage? This predicament is so elemental that, in slightly different guises, it has inspired centuries of literature and popular entertainment, including Daniel Defoe's *Robinson Crusoe* (1719), William Golding's *The Lord of the Flies* (1954), the truly classic *Gilligan's Island* (1964–1967), and more recently, the CBS hit *Survivor*. The underlying question "How will they manage?" fascinates us because it is an allegory that touches upon the very fabric of our economic and social structure.

THE ECONOMIC PROBLEM

Like the group of survivors on *Lost*, every society must decide how to use its limited resources in order to acquire the things that it wants and needs. This is the fundamental economic problem of **scarcity**: How should we allocate scarce resources between alternative uses? Traditionally, economists have broken economic resources into three broad categories known as the **factors of production**: labor, capital, and land.

- **Labor** consists of the time and effort people put into producing goods and services. It is often broken down into "raw" or unskilled labor, which requires no particular skill, and skilled labor, which is the product of training and education. Technological change seems to be raising the demand for skilled labor, causing the wages and salaries of skilled workers to increase relative to those of unskilled workers. So stay in school!
- **Capital** is any asset that yields ongoing benefits over time. It is most commonly interpreted as physical capital, meaning the machinery and tools used to produce goods and services. However, people also accumulate human capital—a stock of skills and knowledge— through training and education. The distinction is vital in the modern economy because, according to some estimates, human capital may actually represent from 60 to 90 percent of our total capital stock. By going to school you are investing in your own human capital.
- **Land** is a catch-all term for all non-reproducible natural resources. Examples include oil, natural gas, and diamonds, but also air and water.

To this list economists sometimes add an amorphous, yet vital fourth factor of production:

- **Entrepreneurship** is the knack for creating and implementing new ideas, even in the face of risk and setbacks. The word comes from the old French verb "entreprendre," which means "to undertake."

Many would argue that the willingness and ability to undertake new ventures is an essential element of the mysterious elixir that sustains long-term growth in the economy.

Every society must decide how it will allocate these scarce factors of production to produce the goods and services it needs. This broad question is in turn commonly broken down into three, more concrete, questions:

- What should be produced? Which goods and services do we want to produce and in what quantities?
- How should the goods and services be produced? What is the best way to use the given resources to achieve the desired production?
- For whom should the goods and services be produced? How should production be shared among the members of society?

ECONOMIC SYSTEMS

Every society must address these questions; there is no escaping them. However, different societies develop different ways of answering them—just as different casts of characters on *Lost* would respond differently to a crash. An **economic system** comprises the ideas and institutions by which a society answers the fundamental economic questions. There are two broad dimensions to an economic system, and these dimensions provide answers to two more questions:

Who Makes the Decisions?

In modern times, there are basically two possibilities. In a **command economy** the economic decisions are made by the government. In a **market economy** the economic decisions are determined in **markets**. A **market** is simply a collection of buyers and sellers who trade something with each other, for a price.

It will be instructive at this point to compare how command and market economies allocate resources. Imagine that a terrible drought kills off most of the orange trees in Florida. In a command economy, the government would have to decide how to curtail the volume or quantity of oranges allocated to different consumers—a daunting logistical and administrative task.

In a market economy, in contrast, the sudden loss of orange trees would reduce the supply of oranges to the market. This would drive up the price of oranges, inducing consumers to reduce the quantity of oranges they want to purchase. In other words, the price increase acts as a signal, telling consumers to adjust their behavior to the new reality of a shortage of oranges. The magical thing about this process is that it happens automatically, and requires no conscious policy decision by the government or anyone else. Prices adjust to induce producers and consumers to respond automatically to changes underlying economic conditions.

The moral of the story is that the market can be a very efficient way of arriving at economic decisions. However, it may not be fair, as poorer people might no longer be able to buy oranges at the higher prices, whereas richer people can continue to buy them.

Who Owns the Factors of Production?

In modern times there have been two answers to this question as well. In a **socialist** economy the factors of production are owned by the state. The pay that people receive for their work is determined by the state, allowing in principle (although rarely in practice) a highly egalitarian distribution of income: As Karl Marx put it in *The Communist Manifesto* (1848), "From each according to his ability, to each according to his needs." In a **capitalist** economy the factors of production are owned by the individuals in the private sector. A worker's pay reflects his or her productivity: "From each according to his ability, to each according to his ability."

In practice socialism is difficult to implement. It requires an absence of envy and jealousy and a concern for the common good, attributes which cannot be realistically expected in most people. It also fails to provide incentives for people to work hard. An old joke in the Soviet Union put it succinctly: A worker was asked about his pay. He shrugged and said, "They pretend to pay us, and we pretend to work." A capitalist system, on the other hand, is built on incentives. Workers have an incentive to work hard; the owners of capital have an incentive to invest it in its most productive uses; entrepreneurs have an incentive to explore new markets and invent new technologies and new goods. In *Capitalism and Freedom* (1962) Nobel laureate Milton Friedman also argued that economic liberty is inextricably linked with political freedom. From this perspective, market capitalism has advantages other than economic over a planned economy.

Economic Systems Around the World

Table 1.1 depicts the possible combinations of ownership and decision making. The combination of a command economy and state ownership is called "centrally planned socialism." Since the collapse of the Soviet Union there are not many countries that operate under this economic system; the only examples today are North Korea and Cuba, and it is unlikely that the system will last too much longer in these countries or resurface anywhere else.

The combination of a market economy with state ownership is "Market Socialism." There were short-lived attempts in this direction in Hungary and Yugoslavia in the 1950s and 1960s.

TABLE 1.1
Ownership and Decision Making

	Market	Command
Private	Market Capitalism	Centrally Planned Capitalism
State	Market Socialism	Centrally Planned Socialism

"Centrally planned capitalism" is the intersection of private ownership with state planning. This might describe the economic system of Sweden or Japan, or even the United States in the middle of World War II.

"Market capitalism" is the combination of markets with private ownership. Although we are accustomed to seeing the government playing an active role in our economic affairs, the United States is probably the closest approximation to a pure market economy in the world today. France and Germany are probably somewhere to the southeast of the United States in the upper left-hand box (market capitalism) in Table 1.1. China is even further to the southeast in this box, or maybe even somewhere in the lower right-hand (centrally planned socialism) box. With the collapse of the Soviet Union in the 1990s, however, it is safe to say that market capitalism has become the dominant economic model on the world stage. This may change. Since the recent financial crisis there has been talk of a new, "Beijing" model for developing countries, one that relies upon much greater state intervention and ownership than is currently seen in the United States.

THE IMPORTANCE OF BUSINESS

In a market capitalist economy the consumer is king. By and large—if we ignore for the moment the constraints imposed by government regulations—consumers have the freedom to purchase the goods they want; they have the freedom to work where they want; they have the freedom to invest their savings in the assets they want. *Businesses are the institutions in a market economy that form the essential link between factors of production and consumers.* This link is often depicted with the famous **circular flow diagram** shown in Figure 1.1.

The counterclockwise flow in the figure shows how consumers (who ultimately own everything in a capitalist economy) provide factors of production (land, labor, and capital) to firms, which use the factors to produce goods and services enjoyed by consumers. The clockwise flow shows the flow of payments between consumers and firms: Consumers spend money on the goods and

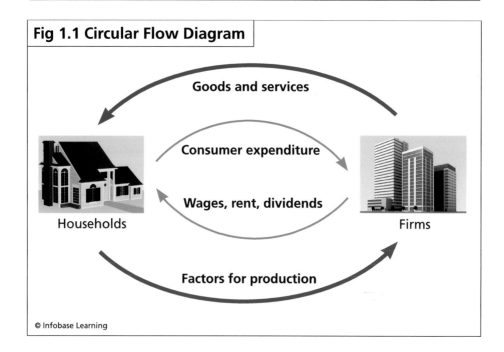

Fig 1.1 Circular Flow Diagram

Goods and services

Consumer expenditure

Wages, rent, dividends

Households

Firms

Factors for production

© Infobase Learning

services, which constitutes **revenue** from the firms' perspective. Firms pay consumers for the use of their factors. They pay **rent** for land, **wages** to labor, and **interest** to capital, all of which constitute **costs** from the firms' perspective. The residual left over after paying costs is **profit** to entrepreneurs. We will have a lot more to say about profit later in this book.

As Figure 1.1 clearly illustrates, businesses serve several vital functions:

- They produce the goods and services that people consume.
- They produce these goods and services by acquiring and employing the factors of production owned by consumers. Businesses hire people as workers, rent the services of land, and invest in capital accumulation by borrowing from consumers.
- Entrepreneurs also hunt for better, cheaper ways of satisfying the needs and wants of consumers, and sometimes invent needs and wants that consumers did not even know they had. The business sector is the creative force behind the innovation and research and development that ultimately drives the long-term growth of the economy.

Business lies at the heart of American society, and not just because it operates at the intersection of the economic activities of production and consumption. It is also the mechanism by which we arrive at most of our fundamental economic decisions, and the creative cauldron from which emerge many of our newest ideas and inventions.

The Evolution of American Business
Now let us briefly consider the evolution of American business. It can conveniently be broken down into several phases, corresponding to or influenced by historical circumstances or technological innovations.

Throughout the colonial period and the early years of the Republic the economy was mostly agricultural. We exported agricultural goods to England in exchange for its manufactured goods. Industrial production was low; firms were small, and self-employment was common.

The first half of the 19th century laid the foundations of the industrial expansion that was to characterize the second half of the century. In the North, there was much investment in infrastructure, such as roads and canals; industry began to take off, and cities grew. People from this region began moving into the rich farmlands of the Midwest. In the South, however, the economy remained predominantly rural and agricultural. Eli Whitney's invention of the cotton gin in 1793 led to rapid growth in cotton production throughout the South, mostly on large plantations using slave labor. In both parts of the country railroads grew rapidly; they were the first really large firms and set an example for the management of the large firms that were to follow.

The victory of the North in the Civil War set the course of the economy for the rest of the century. Slavery was abolished, but the South remained for the most part poor and agricultural. Meanwhile, industry in the North grew rapidly.

In the second half of the 19th century, industry grew apace as firms exploited the power of mass production, allowing large firms to enjoy **economies of scale** (the tendency for per unit costs to decrease with the size of the firm). It was also a time of extraordinary innovation, with the invention and eventually the common use of the telephone, the typewriter, the light-bulb, the telephone, and the automobile. Mark Twain branded this era the "Gilded Age" because of the fabulously wealthy businessmen who came to dominate it. Some of the legendary entrepreneurs of this period included Andrew Carnegie (steel), Jay Gould (railroads), John D. Rockefeller (oil), Cornelius Vanderbilt (steamboats and railroads), and later Henry Ford (cars). In response to what some saw as the excesses of capitalism, the period also gave birth to the American labor movement (in particular the creation of the American Federation of Labor) and the growth of the Populist Party, which was committed to protecting agricultural interests at the expense of industrial interests.

Opposition to unregulated capitalism was enshrined in policy during the Progressive Era, at the end of the 19th and beginning of the 20th century. This period saw the first large-scale regulation of the economy by the government.

Anti-trust law was established with the Sherman Anti-trust Act of 1890; various regulatory agencies that are still with us were created, in particular the Interstate Commerce Commission and the Federal Trade Commission. After a banking panic in 1907, the Federal Reserve System was created in 1913 to implement monetary policy (about which we will have more to say in Chapter 4).

The "roaring" 1920s were characterized by a period of prosperity that you may have encountered in reading the novels of F. Scott Fitzgerald: This was the world of Gatsby. Economic growth spawned a **bubble** (a situation where asset prices continue to increase just because they are expected to increase and not because the true, fundamental value of the assets has changed) in the real estate and stock markets.

The party came to end when the Stock Market crashed in October 1929. The crash was followed by a banking panic in 1930 and the onset of the **Great Depression**. The Depression seems to have been caused by a decline in the aggregate demand for goods and services, perhaps worsened by foolish monetary policy. It marks a watershed in American economic history. At its worst point, 25 percent of the labor force was unemployed! It lasted in essence until the beginning of World War II and forever changed the role of the government in the economy. For the first time the government employed expansionary **fiscal policy** (using deficit spending to stimulate the economy). More broadly speaking, the government for the first time accepted responsibility for controlling the fluctuations in production and employment known as the **business cycle**. At the same time the government tightened the regulation of banking and the financial markets and created the Social Security System as a means of ensuring the well-being of retirees.

The role of the government was reinforced during World War II. The government intervened in markets by implementing price controls and was actively engaged in directing resources to support the war effort. This was the first time that the government became directly involved in making decisions about the allocation of resources.

The post-war years up until the early 1970s were sunny days for the economy. Economic growth was strong; more and more people made it into the middle class. The role of government in the economy continued to grow: By the 1960s the government was firmly committed to "activist" monetary and fiscal policies to manage the aggregate economy; it created sweeping new "social" programs like Medicare and Medicaid; and it spent more money on defense expenditures as part of the Cold War and in particular on the war in Vietnam.

The increase in government expenditures ultimately led to an expansionary monetary policy that fueled **inflation** (an overall increase in prices across the economy). The economy was also hurt when the Organization of Petroleum Exporting States (OPEC) raised oil prices, which increased costs of production and contributed to inflation. The United States found itself suffering from "stagflation," a combination of high inflation and high unemployment. This period also saw a great expansion of the sphere of government regulation, with the creation of the Occupational Safety and Health Administration (OSHA) and the Consumer Product Safety Commission (CPSC).

The 1980s saw a fundamental change in the economy, for two reasons. The Federal Reserve decided to put an end to the inflation by tightening money growth. This induced a severe recession. At about the same time, Ronald Reagan, who had a radically different view of the government in society from his predecessors, was elected President. "Government is not the solution to our problem," he quipped in his first inaugural address, "it *is* the problem." He advocated, and implemented, substantial tax cuts. He also implemented sweeping deregulatory reforms.

The period from the early 1980s until about 2007 is known as the **Great Moderation**, in contrast to the **Great Inflation** the preceded it. Over this time the economy grew strongly and inflation remained under control. The 1990s in particular enjoyed an unprecedented increase in productivity, probably caused by technological innovation and the increased use of the Internet. The Soviet Union fell, and it seemed that market capitalism had become the world's dominant economic model, once and for all. There were, however, signs of trouble. Government debt was growing while private savings fell. The stock market and real estate market were caught in what in retrospect seem clearly to have been dangerously self-fulfilling bubbles.

All this came to an abrupt end with a financial crisis eerily reminiscent of the crash of 1929. The collapse of the "subprime" mortgage market at the beginning of 2007 spread to the real estate market. Banks, hedge funds, and other financial institutions who had invested vast sums in these "toxic" assets were threatened. Some went bankrupt. As the financial markets froze up, the economy slipped into a deep recession, now called the **Great Recession**. The government intervened to support the financial system with massive bailouts; it actually bought shares in some large banks. The government also implemented new, aggressive monetary and fiscal policies to support demand for goods and services. These policies may have created their own problems, however. Today, the government debt is at unprecedented levels, and the bailouts have inserted the government into the private sector in new ways. The response to the Great Recession may represent as much of a shift in the role of the government in the economy as did its response to the Depression, and the long-term effects of this shift are yet to be seen.

Recent Trends in American Business

We have seen how much American business has changed in the last two centuries. However, there are those who argue that American business is now embarked on a transition as dramatic as anything that has happened in history. The sea change is the result of several interrelated forces:

- *Technology.* Advances in computer technology and the Internet have changed the face of business in many ways. Computerized

Computers and the Internet have helped make companies more efficient. In this image, a worker keeps track of shipping inventory using a tracking device. *(Shutterstock)*

inventory management has reduced the need for inventories and facilitated **just-in-time production.** It has also streamlined office red tape and stimulated the use of automated machinery in production. The Internet offers an entirely new way of communicating with both customers and suppliers.

- *Relationships.* Traditionally, firms sought to sell *things* to customers; they practiced "transactions management," producing goods for sale to consumers. Now, many firms have realized that there are huge benefits to be had from hanging on to their customers for extended periods. Instead of selling things, they practice **relationship management** by providing a bundle of services that will nurture a long-term relationship between the company and consumers that purchase its products. The practice, like many others, is facilitated by the use of the Internet, which not only reduces the costs of interacting with customers, but also allows them to exploit the linkages of social-networking sites.

- *Services.* Over the last half-century or so the United States has become a **post-industrial economy.** This means that services have represented a larger and larger share of production—now more than 80 percent. This is partly due to the fact that people have more to spend as incomes have increased. It is also partly due to demographic factors: The aging population requires more health services, for example. People also need professional advice (with questions ranging from how to fill out tax returns to how to use new technologies), advice that can now be found much more easily than before on the Internet.

- *Globalization.* This is shorthand for the increased integration of the U.S. economy with the economies of the rest of the world. It has two principle dimensions. One is increased trade in goods and services with other countries. The growth has been striking: In 1980, for example, exports and imports each represented less than 5 percent of our Gross Domestic Product (GDP, a measure of the total value of production in our economy, which we look at more closely later); today exports are about 17 percent of our GDP, whereas imports are more than 10 percent. This is a small change relative to that experienced in other countries, but it represents a dramatic increase for the United States, one that is sure to continue as growth in other countries (in particular China and India) accelerates. The export sector is the one part of the economy that is doing well in the current crisis. In turn, much of the growth in our exports is due to our service sector. The other dimension of globalization is financial. It is now possible to buy and sell financial assets all around the globe;

this is made easier because of the Internet, which not only facilitates rapid communication but also makes it easier to acquire information about investments (and investment opportunities) in other countries. Most of our government debt is held by people (and central banks) in other countries; much of the splurge in our consumption prior to this last crisis was financed by borrowing from abroad.

WHAT THIS BOOK IS ABOUT

This chapter addressed the broad philosophical question of what businesses do in a market capitalist system. Hopefully it included enough about the evolution of American business to convince you of its central role in our society. Business affects, and is affected by, technological innovation and economic growth. It seems to change as the government responds to the perceived excesses or inadequacies of capitalism.

But now that you have the big picture, you are probably anxious to get down to the nitty-gritty questions of how the world of business actually works, and how—perhaps the most pressing subject—you might fit into it. That is what defines the content and purpose of this book. On the one hand, it serves as a primer on American business, sketching the basic concepts and providing the basic facts needed to make educated choices in the business world. On the other, it also provides practical information about starting your own business. And who knows? Maybe what you discover in these pages will help you become the next Bill Gates or Steve Jobs.

Here is our plan of attack: The first part of the book (Chapter 2, 3, and 4) provides a survey of the business world. Chapter 2 examines the basic decision-making and organizational unit of the business, the **firm**. We discuss different types of firms and their legal properties. We focus in particular on the **corporation**, one of the greatest economic innovations in history. The corporation creates a wedge between the owners and managers of the firm. This in turn creates the need for **corporate governance**, which is the art of getting managers to do what they are supposed to do for the owners.

Chapter 3 examines what it is, exactly, that firms try to do. This leads us to the fundamental notion of **profit** and the principle of **value maximization** of stockholders. The chapter explains the fundamental role of profits in stimulating innovation and directing resources to their most productive uses. However, it also considers the responsibility of the firm to serve not only stockholders but also other **stakeholders.**

Chapter 4 considers the external environment impinging on the firm. This environment is two-pronged. The *macroeconomic environment* constitutes the things that are happening to the economy as a whole. Examples include economic growth, unemployment, interest rates, and exchange rates, as well as government policies that affect them. The *microeconomic environment* depends upon the nature of the markets in which a firm operates, in particular the degree and nature of competition in those markets.

The second half of the book steps away from the business world as a whole to look at the practical question of how you, the budding entrepreneur, might get started in creating your own business. Chapter 5 looks at the decision to go into business for oneself. It summarizes the attributes of successful entrepreneurs so you can better assess whether this endeavor is suited to you. It also looks at ways of assessing the viability of your business ideas by using **market research**, determining the potential demand for what you want to sell.

Chapter 6 looks at the mechanics of starting a business. It discusses how to market your product, how to estimate your costs and profitability, how to get financing, and how to write a business plan. Presuming that you have enjoyed some initial success, Chapter 7 then discusses how to expand your company, a critical point in the growth of the firm, which has legal and financial dimensions as well as implications for how your product is marketed.

Further Reading

Boder, S. *Capitalizing on Change: A Social History of American Business*. Chapel Hill, North Carolina: University of North Carolina Press, 2009.

Friedman, M. *Capitalism and Freedom*. Chicago: University of Chicago Press, 1962.

Mankiw, N.G. *Principles of Economics*. 6th ed. Mason, Ohio: South-Western Publishing Company, 2012.

Marx, K., and F. Engels. *The Communist Manifesto*. 1848. Introduction by Martin Malia. New York: Penguin, reprinted 1998.

Smith, A. *An Inquiry into the Nature and Causes of the Wealth of Nations*. 1776. Chicago: University of Chicago Press, reprinted 1977.

CHAPTER 2

THE FIRM

. . . the firm is a nexus of contracts . . .
—Michael Jensen and William Meckling

Corporation: An ingenious device for
obtaining profit without individual responsibility.
—Ambrose Bierce

The fundamental decision-making unit of business is the **firm**, and this chapter addresses some basic questions about this entity: What exactly is a firm? What are the legal forms that firms might assume, and what are the advantages and disadvantages of each? Particular attention is focused on the legal entity known as the **corporation.** Among other issues, this chapter explains how corporations join together, or **merge**, and the concept of **corporate governance**, the art of inducing managers to do what they are supposed to do.

THE NATURE OF THE FIRM
Our inquiry on this subject begins with a question that may at first glance seem odd: Why do firms exist at all? This question has deep implications, leading to an even more puzzling question: How do firms fit in with our understanding of markets and how they function?

In Chapter 1 you read that markets allocate resources much more efficiently than central planners. But *within* a firm the decisions about how to allocate resources are made by a "central planner"—otherwise known as "the boss." If you can visualize this as small and large islands of central planning (firms) scattered about a vast sea of decentralized decision making (markets), you can grasp this concept pretty easily. So how can we explain this paradox?

Nobel laureate Ronald Coase posed this same question about the reason for the existence of firms in a now famous article published in 1937. Coase's brilliant insight was that there are costs associated with making market transactions. These **transactions costs** take a variety of forms. It takes time and money to discover a trading partner. Then it takes time and money to negotiate a deal and to pay lawyers to draw up a contract. Finally, it takes time and money to monitor trading partners to make sure that they do what they are supposed to, and to enforce the contract if they do not. Coase argued that when transactions costs are sufficiently high, it pays to create an institution that precludes or greatly reduces these costs. That institution is the firm.

Suppose, for example, that you wanted a bicycle. In principle, you could buy all of the parts yourself and pay individual contractors to assemble them for you. Think of how much time you would spend looking for all of the parts, assuring the quality of each, finding someone able to put the bike together, and drafting a contract to ensure that he or she would do the job right. How much easier it is to have this entity called the firm that does all the work described above and guarantees the outcome.

As noted above, decisions within the firm are made centrally, by the boss, rather than through market mechanisms. Some would argue, however, that Coase may have overemphasized and oversimplified the coercive aspect of the firm—i.e., it avoids the costs of the market because the boss tells everyone in the firm what to do, without wasting time and money searching and negotiating. These critics posit that everyone involved in the firm does so willingly. You may not agree with what the boss says to do, but you are always free to quit. Of course, being free to lose your job is perilously close to coercion. Nonetheless anytime you accept a job, you are implicitly agreeing to be coerced (within limits of course) and are expected to operate within certain fixed guidelines set by the boss.

A more modern view of the firm than the one promulgated by Coase was proposed by Michael Jensen (another Nobel laureate) and William Meckling. These economists defined the basic nature of a firm as a "nexus of contracts," implicit and explicit, that organizes the way owners, managers, and employees operate as a unit.

A few paragraph above, we discussed the concept of transaction costs, which are likely to be much higher and more onerous for an individual than for a firm. Firms may also have an advantage over the market when there are **specific**

assets to deal with. A specific asset is one that has only one specific use. Returning to our bicycle example, suppose that the company's bicycles are designed to include a special sprocket that can only be produced by one machine and that this machine can produce nothing else. Obviously, very few individuals could afford to invest in such a machine. The bicycle company might also hesitate before making this kind of investment. The bicycle company could, however, subcontract the production of the sprocket to another firm that makes sprockets (a so-called "downstream supplier"), but this might not work and might give rise to unwanted complications. The bicycle company might not trust the supplier to provide quality sprockets or the desired quantity of sprockets on time, or the subcontractor might insist on locking into a long-term contract. But a long-term contract could make both parties uneasy: If the supplier were the only source of sprockets, it could try to extort the bicycle company by demanding higher payments. Conversely, if the bicycle company were the only firm using the supplier's sprockets it could try to extort the supplier by demanding lower payments once it had invested in the capital to make its sprockets. Or both firms could pay lawyers lots of money to devise contracts to avoid being extorted by each other. The obvious solution is for the supplier and the firm to merge to create a single firm, a move that precludes the contracting costs of the market for both.

Although firms exist to avoid or reduce the transactions costs of the market, it is important to remember that there are also important contracting costs *within* each firm. These arise from the fact that individuals associated with the firm may be self-interested and so may not act in its best interest. For one thing, workers may simply not want to work as hard they are expected to work. Another classic example is what may happen when a firm's owner and a firm's management have divergent views on how things should work. The manager is supposed to act as the "agent" of the owner, running the firm in a manner that maximizes the returns to the owner. But because the manager does not have a stake in the firm himself, he may engage in a variety of dysfunctional behaviors, such as providing himself extra perks (a larger office, or trips to Paris), or investing in assets that are too risky, or simply shirk responsibilities that are part of the management position. To overcome this **agency problem**, it becomes necessary to organize the firm to provide incentives for the manager to work in the interests of the owner. This is the province of corporate governance, which we will discuss in more detail at the end of this chapter.

It is important to understand that firms facing different types of transactions costs are likely to behave in different ways. From the perspective of the social scientist, this understanding provides a framework around which to devise theories about how firms look and behave. In the "Darwinian" world of business, where only the "fittest," most efficient firms survive in the long run, the form, organization, and behavior of firms should evolve to minimize transaction costs in a given economic environment. This is the underlying premise of the modern economic theory of the firm. In other words, it helps explain *what firms actually do*. In particular, it may offer insights into the way a particular industry works. Moreover, understanding environmental and transactional distinctions among firms may hold important lessons for the budding entrepreneur: It may suggest *what you should do*, providing clues to the form your firm should take and how it should be organized. An efficient form and organization will reduce your costs, and raise your profits.

LEGAL FORMS OF FIRMS

Having answered the question of why firms exist, we can move on to address the overarching issue of how they exist. This section enumerates the different legal forms that firms can take. It also explains the costs and benefits and advantages and disadvantages of the various forms.

Profit versus Non-profit

The first way of classifying firms is according to their legal profit status. Non-profit firms constitute only about 6 percent of the firms in the United States but provide a wide range of important social services. Most non-profit firms are either charitable, religious, or social service organizations. The legal definition of "non-profit," however, is simply that the people running the firm do not receive its residual profits. This does *not* mean that the firm cannot make profits (in the sense that revenue exceeds cost); only that the profits cannot be redistributed. Instead they must be reinvested or held as retained earnings. In fact, although most non-profits are expressly created to achieve objectives other than maximizing profits, there is nothing to prevent a non-profit from trying to maximize profits. Indeed, for-profit and non-profit firms sometimes compete in the same sectors (think of hospitals or universities), and it is an open question as to whether their behaviors differ in any discernable way.

Suppose you are thinking of starting a business. Should you file for non-profit or for-profit status? What are the advantages and disadvantages of each? The main advantage of non-profit status is that it provides exemption from most state, local, and federal taxes. This status provides the additional advantage of attracting monetary donations and volunteers. The prohibition against paying out profits means that people are more likely to trust that their donations of time and money will be used for good purposes. Furthermore, donations to a non-profit business are tax deductible. The main disadvantage is that the prohibition against paying out profits makes it harder to finance investments. The non-profit firm cannot issue stock, so it can pay for its investments only by using its retained earnings, issuing debt, or attracting donations.

Types of For-profit Firms

The traditional taxonomy of for-profit firms includes three distinct structures: sole proprietorship, partnership, and corporation. Each of these is defined and explained below along with an overview of advantages and disadvantages.

Sole Proprietorship

The **sole proprietorship** is the most basic and most prevalent type of firm and constitutes 72 percent of all firms. As the name suggests, a sole proprietorship is a firm owned by a single individual, so he or she has complete decision-making authority and the right to all residual profits.

Sole proprietorship has several advantages. First, it is easy to set up, usually requiring nothing more than a local business license. Second, since the owner *is* the manager there is no agency problem. Third, the firm itself is not taxed; instead the tax is "passed through" directly to the owner's personal income tax liability. To these advantages, some would add the intangible benefit of being your own boss, and making your own decisions.

The most serious disadvantage of the sole proprietorship is that comes with **unlimited liability.** The owner is personally responsible for all debts of the firm and can be held personally liable if someone sues. Other limitations are that it is typically hard for a sole proprietor to borrow large amounts money to finance his or her investments, and that the firm "dies" (unless bequeathed to someone else) when the owner dies. Furthermore, being your own boss is a two-edged sword: You get to make your own decisions, but it can prevent you from utilizing the skills and expertise of others.

Partnerships

Partnerships are firms that are owned and managed jointly by more than one person. They constitute 8 percent of all firms and come in several flavors. In a **general partnership** all partners are treated equally by law and are equally liable for debts. In a **limited partnership** some of the partners are named "general partners" and are responsible for operating the firm. The other partners are named "limited partners." They collect a share of profits but play no active role in operations and are liable only up to the amount of their respective investment in the firm. Some states now recognize **limited liability partnerships** (LLPs), where all partners have limited liability. The LLP is often favored by groups of doctors, lawyers, and accountants because it limits the extent to which a suit against one member of the group can damage the others.

The first advantage of a partnership is the same as that of a sole proprietorship: It is easy to set up. The second is that it allows the firm to avail itself of the skills of more than one person. This in turn may make it easier to borrow money, because lenders might see the broader skill base as less risky than the one-person skill base of a sole proprietor. Having more initial investors may also increase the initial capital available to the firm.

The principle disadvantage of partnership (except for LLPs) is also the same as that for sole proprietorship, namely unlimited liability. The other problem is the flip side of having a broader set of skills—to borrow from a well-known adage, having more than one cook may ruin the soup. In addition, there is always the possibility of personality clashes and differences of opinion. Another tricky problem that can surface is having to deal with a **free rider**, someone who just doesn't do his or her share of the work (think of your experience in group projects).

Corporation

A **corporation** is what lawyers call a "false person" (as opposed to a "natural person" like you or me). Corporations constitute about 20 percent of all firms. Being a corporation means that a firm can own property, engage in contracts, and (in general) practice business just like a real person. A corporation is required to have a **board of directors**, a group of individuals who jointly make most of the major strategic decisions for the firm. A corporation also has the ability to issue **stock.**

Stockholders are the owners of the corporation. In exchange for owning a share of the firm, every stockholder may receive a share of profits called a **dividend** (note, however, that firms are not obligated to pay dividends). A stockholder's rights depend upon the type of stock he or she owns. **Common stock** confers voting rights, one vote per share. Holders of common stock normally have the right to vote on some important decisions being considered by the firm and to elect the board of directors. **Preferred stock** usually does not confer voting rights. However, preferred stock has two advantages over common stock. First, owners of preferred stock have prior claim to the firm's assets (that is, before owners of common stock) if the firm goes under. (The order of priority in claiming the firm's assets follows this sequence: creditors first, preferred stock holders second, and common stock holders last). The second advantage is that preferred stockholders also receive their dividends before common stockholders do.

Corporations have two very important advantages. The first is that stockholders have only limited liability, so that they can lose only the amount that they invest in the firm. This follows from the fact that the firm is legally distinct from its owners. The second advantage is liquidity. If the firm's stock is traded, stockholders can easily sell their shares for cash. In contrast, the assets of proprietorships and partnerships may be quite illiquid. These two features together make the corporation much more attractive to investors than either proprietorships or partnerships. Incorporating a firm is therefore a powerful way of garnering external investment capital. In fact, it can be argued that the invention of the modern corporation in the 19th century was one of the key innovations in the evolution of capitalism. It permitted the large firms of that era—especially railroads, steel, and heavy industry—to acquire the enormous amounts of capital need to nurture their growth. It is still an essential tool in the acquisition of capital for large and growing firms.

Corporations also have disadvantages. First, setting up a corporation is costly and complex. Second, most corporations suffer from **double taxation.** As a distinct "person" the corporation is first subject to state and federal corporate income taxes. Stockholders are then also liable for income taxes on dividends paid out by the firm. Last, but not least, the separation of ownership from management may create severe agency problems. How can the owners of the firm ensure that the managers act in their best interest?

TYPES OF CORPORATIONS

Corporations are not identical. They can usefully be categorized into classes according to the answers to two questions: Who owns the stock? and How is the firm taxed?

Who Owns the Stock?

A corporation can be either **closely held** or **publicly traded**. The stock of closely held (or "closed") corporations is held by a small number of people (often a family) and is not traded. The stock of publicly traded firms is offered for sale to the general public and is often traded on large, organized exchanges such as the New York Stock Exchange. One advantage for corporations with closely held stock is that it seems to reduce the agency problem. Although personality conflicts and family in-fighting among the small number of owners may exist, the owners in essence are the managers and do not have to contend with "outsider" issues. One disadvantage of operating as a closely held stock corporation is that it restricts access to capital. To finance investments the owners have to either use their retained earnings or issue debt.

How Is the Firm Taxed?

As noted above, corporations are taxed twice, once through the corporate income tax and then through the personal income tax. Actually, the issue of double taxation is a bit more complicated than this explanation may suggest. Most corporations are **C corporations** (creatively named after Subsection C of Chapter 1 of the Internal Revenue Code). They are taxed twice but face no restrictions on either how much stock they can issue or who can purchase the stock. **S corporations** (you guessed it, Subsection S of Chapter 1 of the Internal Revenue Code) have a tax advantage over C corporations at the federal level. They face no corporate income tax, so income is passed through and is only taxed as personal income. In essence, S corporations enjoy both the tax advantages of proprietorships and partnerships and the benefits of being corporations (limited liability and the ability to issue stock). The S corporation was created to help stimulate small businesses, so firms aspiring to this status must satisfy rather restrictive conditions. First, there can be no more than 75 stockholders. Second, the firm must be incorporated in the United States. Third, there can only be a single class of stock.

GETTING TOGETHER: MERGERS AND ACQUISITIONS

The opening sections of this chapter touched on the subject of mergers, particularly as a means of dealing with production of something that a firm uses in its main product but has no interest in producing that something itself, generally because doing so would require investing in capital that cannot be used for other purposes. This, however, is only one of several reasons firms get together. This section addresses other reasons and examines the merger/acquisition process.

How Do Firms Join Together?

Firms can join forces through mergers and acquisitions (M&As). The distinction between a merger and an acquisition is actually rather murky.

- Legally, a **merger** occurs when two firms agree to create a new entity. Stockholders in both firms surrender their shares in exchange for shares in the new firm.
- An **acquisition** occurs when one firm purchases another. The stockholders of one firm purchase the shares held by the stockholders of the other company in order to acquire a controlling interest. Facebook recently bought a small company called Divvyshot, a new firm that provides a group-sharing Website for photos, an example of a rather cheap acquisition.
- One occasionally hears of **consolidations** (or consolidation mergers), where a newly created company buys the shares of the once independent companies that have come together to form a new, or consolidated, company.

In common parlance, mergers and acquisitions are often treated as synonyms (in fact, acquisitions are sometimes called "purchase mergers"). The crucial, practical distinction is whether the joining of the firms is "friendly" or "hostile." A merger is almost by definition *friendly*, because it occurs when the stockholders and management of both firms involved agree that the union of the two firms is desirable. An acquisition, on the other hand, involves an attempt by one firm to take over another. It may be friendly, or it may be a **hostile takeover bid**. If the bid is friendly, the management of the selling firm supports it and advises its stockholders to accept it. Facebook's acquisition of Divvyshot was friendly.

If the bid is hostile, the management of the selling firm opposes it. To succeed in a hostile takeover bid, the buying firm must convince enough of the stockholders of the selling firm to surrender their shares, thus allowing it to acquire a controlling interest. To encourage this surrender of shares, the firm may offer stockholders cash or shares in the company that will emerge once the takeover occurs. Sometimes the buying firm sells bonds (issues debt) as a way of acquiring the funds needed to purchase the shares of the selling firm. This is called a **leveraged buyout**, or LBO ("leverage" in this context essentially means debt). In theory this debt can be paid off either with the acquired firm's revenues or by selling the acquired firm's assets. In practice though, LBOs can be dangerous because paying off the interest and principal on the debt may make it harder to finance operations or investment. LBOs were the weapon of choice of the famous corporate raiders of the 1980s, such as Carl Icahn and T. Boone Pickens, but they were also used extensively in a wave of large acquisitions in the run up to the financial crisis of 2008.

Types of Mergers
Henceforth we will use the generic term "merger" to refer both to mergers and to acquisitions proper, because they have the same economic effects. That said, mergers are traditionally broken down into four categories:

- A **vertical merger** is the joining of a firm and one of its suppliers. An example of this was cited at the beginning of this chapter, where the bicycle company bought the sprocket producer. A real-world example was the merger between the cable operator Time Warner Incorporated and Turner Corporation, which produces CNN and TBS.
- A **horizontal merger** occurs between two firms that provide the same good or service in the same market. If the bicycle firm in our example were to buy out another bicycle firm down the street, it would be a horizontal merger. A good real-world example was the attempt by Staples, the office supply chain, to buy out Office Depot. Anti-trust regulators look closely at horizontal mergers because they may reduce competition; they prevented the merger of Staples with Office Depot.
- A **conglomeration merger** joins two firms producing unrelated goods or services. A good example is General Electric (GE). As its name suggests, GE got its start producing electrical goods; however, it has diversified into financial services and now owns the National Broadcasting Company (NBC).

When it was founded in 1892 by Thomas Edison, General Electric was focused solely on energy and electrical appliances. Today GE is a multinational conglomerate with divisions in finance, media, aviation and other enterprises. *(Photo by Jud McCranie. Wikipedia)*

- A **market extension merger** occurs when a company expands to sell its goods or services in new geographical locations. This might happen if our bicycle company were to open a new store in another city. An important real-world example is the banking industry. Prior to 1994, interstate banking was prohibited by federal law (although there were already many ways of circumventing it). After interstate banking was legalized, there was a wave of mergers of banks as they moved across state borders.
- A **product extension merger** involves companies that provide different but *related* goods or services. An example of this might be that our bicycle company also decides to sell small, fuel-efficient

motor-scooters (like Vespas). The purchase of Divvyshot by Facebook is a real-world example.

Why Merge?

Firms merge for many reasons, but the overarching incentive is that one or both firms involved stand to gain from doing so. Indeed, firms contemplating a merge are likely to perceive a number of benefits from joining together. These potential benefits are generically known as **synergies**. An assortment of benefits falling into this broad classification is presented in the accompanying sidebar.

There are also downsides to mergers. The acquisition of another firm, for example, may impose high costs of paying off the interest and principal of the

Synergies: Why Firms Merge

Economies of scale. This occurs when an increase in the scale (size) of operations permits a lower cost per unit. A merger may allow redundant positions, units, or plants to be shut down. Indeed, mergers are often associated with **layoffs**.

Economies of scope. Suppose that two companies each initially produce one good. They merge to form a bigger firm. There are economies of scope if it costs less for the new, big firm to produce *both* goods together than it would be for the individual companies to produce them separately. Economies of scope normally arise through efficiencies in either advertising or distribution: It might be cheaper to have one sales force market both goods, for example, or to distribute both goods using one truck fleet.

New Technology. Acquiring another firm may provide access to new technologies. Facebook's purchase of Divvyshot may be seen in this light.

Cross-selling. A merger may also increase revenues by encouraging **cross-selling**. When General Motors (GM) got into the automobile financing business, for example, it raised the demand for GM's cars by making it easier for consumers to get credit. Conversely, the increased sales of GM's cars created the demand for its financing wing.

Diversification. This is sometimes a justification for conglomerate merger. The idea is that by selling two goods, for example, it is possible to diversify risk because the demand for one of the goods may be up when the demand for other is down. However, the reality is that it is much less costly for investors to diversify their portfolios of financial assets themselves than for the firm to increase the value of the firm by diversifying.

debt issued to finance it. Some firms, in fact, are too eager to jump into mergers, overestimating the advantages thereof, particularly during times when credit is cheap.

Another problem may arise from diseconomies of scale. As a firm increases in size, it may become more and more difficult to manage. In particular, integrating the operations of firms with different management styles and cultures can be a difficult problem for management. Suppose one firm has a rigid, hierarchical management style and everyone wears button-down shirts, whereas the other has a laid-back management style and everyone wears tie-dyed shirts. Think how hard it would be to get the people coming from these disparate firm cultures to work together.

In some cases, a merger may alienate the customer base. There is some evidence that managers focus so hard on cutting costs after a merger that they forget the revenue side of the business. Service slips and customers abandon the firm.

Finally, mergers may be a symptom of a management style intent on empire building. This may result from the way managers are paid—if their salary depends upon the size of the firm or market share, for example. In other cases, this empire-building tendency may arise sociologically from a propensity of certain managers to measure their success by the size of their firms. It has also been suggested that **hubris** (a Greek word, meaning "excessive pride") may lead managers to consistently overestimate the benefits of mergers.

CORPORATE GOVERNANCE

Corporate governance is all about designing the firm and structuring incentives in a manner that gets management to do what is supposed to do. The overarching question here is who calls the shots on this "supposed to"? We have seen that the owners of a corporation are its stockholders. We have also seen that the corporation is required to have a board of directors, elected by the stockholders. The board normally engages in long-run strategic planning, makes big decisions like whether to pay dividends, and is supposed to oversee the performance of the corporation financially. It also plays a major role in selecting the senior managers of the firm, in particular the **Chief Executive Officer (CEO).** Although it varies from firm to firm, the board is usually not very active in the day to day operations of the company—this is left to the CEO and management. The basic chain of responsibility in the firm can be represented in a simple diagram:

Stockholders → Board of Directors → Management

The Problem

The critical thing to notice about this chain is that the owners of the firm are two steps removed from those who actually manage the firm. This is where the **agency problem** arises. The managers of the firm may look after their own interests, which may not be the same as those of the stockholders. How might the interests of managers deviate from those of owners? For one thing, if their compensation does not depend upon the profitability of the firm, they may have an incentive to give themselves extra perquisites or not work very hard. For another, they have a lot of their own human capital invested in the firm, so they may be more **risk averse** than the stockholders (who can diversify their risk by investing in a range of assets). This means the managers might pass up certain risky investments that could be advantageous to the stockholders.

Solutions

There are two extreme ways of solving the agency problem. On the one hand, we could just make the managers the owners of the firm (as in proprietorship and partnerships). By definition there could be no conflict of interest. But this would be difficult to implement and still reap the benefits of having hundreds or thousands of stockholders from whom to acquire capital. On the other hand, the owners could spend lots of time and money watching over the managers' shoulders to make sure they were doing the right thing. But this would be prohibitively expensive, and might even impair the efficiency of the firm. So in the real world each firm finds its own judicious mix of these two options. Possible variations on this theme are presented below.

- Owners can try to **monitor** the behavior of managers by insisting on transparency of the bookkeeping, by insisting on independent **auditors**, and by prodding the audit committee of the board of directors to keep an eye on things.
- The board itself is supposed to be looking after the interests of the shareholders, but may become captive to the management. For this reason stockholders may insist on the board including "external" members who are not members of the management team.
- The stockholders may become much more active in the decisions of the firm. They could threaten to kick the management and board out, or, less drastically, they could insist on certain decisions being made only with stockholder approval. But these tactics are hard to apply if there are many, many shareholders. Nowadays, however, most stock is not owned by individuals directly, but by **institutional investors** like pension funds, mutual funds, and insurance companies. The sheer size of these companies gives them more weight in influencing boards and mangers. There are examples of CEOs at large corporations being forced to resign because of inadequate performance. However, the growth of institutional investing hasn't been entirely good for corporate governance. Institutional investors

have large, diversified portfolios and so may not be too concerned about the behavior of one firm. Furthermore, if they suspect mismanagement, some feel it may be cheaper to "cut and run" by selling shares of the firm rather than trying to reform it.

- Instead of stricter oversight, stockholders can try to change the incentives of the managers in order to induce them to do the right thing. One way of doing this is to make the managers part owners by issuing them stock for good performance. However, this may make managers too focused on short-term fluctuations in stock prices. Another popular device is to reward managers with stock **options.** A **call option** is a financial contract that confers the right to buy an asset (here a stock) at a given price, called the "strike price." The idea is to give managers an incentive to raise profits, and so increase the price of the stock. If the price of the stock goes above the strike price, the manager can exercise the option to buy the stock at the strike price, then sell it for a profit at the higher price going on the stock market. This is a powerful incentive mechanism, so much so that some firms actually distribute stock options to regular employees as an incentive to work harder.

There is also a powerful external force that can offset the agency problem. If managers do not perform well, the price of a firm's stock may fall. The undervalued stock may provoke a **hostile takeover bid** if a potential buyer thinks it can manage the firm better. In other words, there may be a **market for corporate control**, through which the threat of takeovers provides an incentive for managers to do their jobs properly. There is enormous controversy about whether the market for corporate control is effective in mitigating agency problems.

SUMMARY

This chapter progressed from the philosophical to the immediately practical aspects of business. The philosophical question was why firms exist all. The answer was that putting all of the people and activities required for production in one organization reduces the transactions costs of trading in markets. However, each firm also has internal costs and concerns related to organizing production. Among these is the need to monitor behavior and provide the right incentives so that people do what they are supposed to do. The organization and behavior of firms evolve as a result of efforts to minimize these transactions costs, internal and external. Firms that don't do so won't survive. Different firms act in different ways because they face different economic circumstances and different types of transactions costs.

Moving from the philosophical to the practical, we examined different legal forms that firms can take: sole proprietorships, partnerships, and corporations.

Although sole proprietorships and partnership constitute the vast majority of the firms, most large firms are corporations. We then discussed the means and motives for firms to join through mergers and acquisitions, concluding with a discussion of corporate governance. The corporation is a powerful institution, capable of attracting investors and capital, but it also creates a wedge between owners and managers. The challenge is to organize the corporation so that managers act in the interests of the owners.

Further Reading

Bovée, C., Thrall, J., and M. Mescon. *Excellence in Business.* 3rd ed. Upper Saddle River, N.J.: Pearson, 2007.

Brickley, J., J. Zimmerman, and C. Smith, C. *Managerial Economics & Organizational Architecture.* 5th ed. New York: McGraw-Hill/Irwin, 2008.

Coase, R. "The Nature of the Firm." *Economica* 4 (1937): 386–405.

Jensen, M., and W. Meckling. "Theory of the Firm: Managerial Behavior, Agency Costs and Ownership Structure." *Journal of Financial Economics* 3 (1976): 305–360.

Meiners, R., A. Ringleb, and F. Edwards. *The Legal Environment of Business.* Mason, Ohio: Southwestern Publishing Company, 2000.

Narayanan, M., and V. Nanda. *Finance for Strategic Decision Making: What Non-financial Managers Need to Know.* New York: John Wiley & Sons, 2008.

CHAPTER 3

THE OBJECTIVES OF THE FIRM

... there is one and only one social responsibility of business—to use its resources and engage in activities designed to increase its profits so long as it stays within the rules of the game, which is to say, engages in open and free competition, without deception or fraud.
—Milton Friedman

Making a profit is no more the purpose of a corporation than getting enough to eat is the purpose of life. Getting enough to eat is a requirement of life; life's purpose, one would hope, is somewhat broader and more challenging. Likewise with business and profit.
—Kenneth Mason, founder of Quaker Oats

Chapter 2 provided a rationale for why firms exist at all, described the forms they might take, and emphasized the importance of corporate governance. There has as yet been nothing to explain what businesses do or try to do. What is, or what should be, the objective of the firm? The traditional answer is straightforward: Firms should act in the best interests of their owners. This is often expressed in the assertion that for-profit firms should try to maximize profits! So we begin this chapter by defining profits and assessing their importance in a market capitalist system. Next we relate **profit maximization** to the concept of **value maximization**, a broader and arguably more functional objective than profit maximization. This is based on the premise that the managers of a corporation should try to maximize the price of the firm's stock. Over the last two decades or so, however, the traditional view that the firm should act only in the interests of its owners has come under assault. Critics argue that firms should be concerned not only with the interests of their owners, but also with the interests of other people who are impacted by what firms do. Thus, they argue, a firm's objective should be to maximize value to **stakeholders** in general, not just shareholders. We will examine the specifics of this debate and assess its implications in relation to the practical realities of running a business.

PROFIT

Profits are what you make from selling your good or service after you have paid all your expenses. This is true as far as it goes, but we need to be a bit more precise. In the world of economists, profit is defined by a formula, and each component of that formula stands for something very specific.

$$\text{Profit} = \text{Revenue} - \text{Costs}$$

Revenue

Revenue, or what accountants call **income**, is straight forward. It is the inflow of money coming into the firm. Most revenue comes from the sales of the products or services provided by the firm. As an example, suppose that you are the owner of the bicycle factory first introduced in Chapter 2. If you sell 15 ten-speed bikes per month for $2,500 apiece (it is a very up-scale store) and nothing else, your revenue would be $37,500 (or $2,500 × 15). If you also sold 5 mountain bikes for $5,000 apiece your revenue would be $62,500 (or $2,500 × 15 + $5,000 × 5). You get the idea.

Costs

Costs comprise the dollar value of everything you have to sacrifice to produce what you sell. There is more to this than meets the eye, however, because there are different types of costs, and understanding profit requires an understanding (and distinguishing between) all of the costs involved.

Explicit Costs

Explicit costs are the actual dollars that you expend in producing your goods. Accountants call these **expenditures**. They consist of all the things you normally associate with running a business, such as wages, salaries, rent, and the cost of maintaining or expanding your capital stock. Let's revisit our bicycle factory and look at some specific explicit costs. Suppose that you pay $1,000 in rent per month and employ 5 workers, each of whom works 160 hours per month at a wage of $15 an hour. Your total explicit costs would be $13,000 or $1,000 (rent) + $15 (hourly rate) × 160 (hours worked) × 5 (workers).

The salary of the worker in this photo would be an example of an explicit and variable cost. *(Shutterstock)*

Implicit Costs

Implicit costs are more subtle. They represent what you sacrifice by *not* doing something else with your time and energy. Suppose that before entering the bicycle business you had a successful career as a trial attorney, making a salary of $50,000 a month (you were a *very* good attorney). You left the legal rat race to fulfill a childhood dream of building bicycles. However, by *not* being an attorney you are sacrificing $50,000 a month that you would have earned if you had stayed in the legal rat race. Therefore, the salary you gave up is an implicit extra cost that must be added on to your explicit costs to determine your real costs of running the bicycle factory. Just because they are not tallied up by your accountant does not mean that they are not important.

Variable Costs

Variable costs are costs that increase with (or more generally vary with) the volume of the good that you produce. They typically include things like wages, salaries, and purchases of raw materials. In our bicycle factory example, one variable cost would be your labor cost. Each worker is paid $15 an hour and it takes 5 hours to make a single bicycle. If you wanted to produce another bicycle, your costs would increase by $75 ($15 x 5). Now consider that would happen if your bicycles become so popular that more and more people want to buy them. To produce the needed quantity, you might need to hire more labor. For each additional worker hired, your variable costs increase, because you are paying an additional $15 per hour for every new person hired. An increase in variable costs would also show up in how much you spend on raw materials—you can't make 6 bicycles if you have only 4 wheels in your stockroom.

Fixed Costs

Fixed costs, as the name suggests, are costs that do not vary with how much you produce. They consist of things like rent, insurance contributions, and the cost of maintaining your capital stock. A fixed cost for the bicycle factory is the $1,000 it pays per month for rent.

One very important type of fixed costs is **sunk costs**. These are costs that you have already incurred and which cannot be recovered. Suppose, for example, that you are thinking about opening the bicycle shop, but are not quite sure whether it will be profitable. So instead of simply renting the shop for a flat rate of $1,000 per month, you take out an option to lease. This means that if you do go into business and use the space, you pay the landlord $1,000. However, this arrangement also gives you the option of not using the space, in which case you forfeit a penalty of $200 to the landlord. In this case the sunk cost is $200, because you have irrevocably locked into paying it and cannot recover it; the remaining $800 is a fixed cost that is not sunk, because you can recover it if you do not go into business.

Definitions of Profit

There are two fundamental concepts of profit, corresponding to the concepts of explicit and implicit costs:

> **Accounting profit**, or what accountants call **Net Income** (this includes all explicit costs but no implicit costs):
>
> Accounting Profit = Revenue − Explicit Costs
>
> **Economic profit** includes implicit as well as explicit costs:
>
> Economic Profit = Revenue − Explicit Costs − Implicit Costs

Always remember that it is economic profit that really matters in making your business decisions. The hypothetical numbers we introduced for our bicycle firm may make this clear. Your firm sold 15 ten-speeds for $2,500 apiece and 5 mountain bikes for $5,000 apiece, so we saw that its revenue was $62,500. You

Total Cost

Total cost is the sum of fixed and variable costs:

Cost = Fixed Cost + Variable Cost

paid rent of $1000, and incurred labor costs of $12,000, so your explicit costs were $13,000. This leaves an accounting profit of $49,500 = $62,500 - $13,000, so it looks like you doing pretty well.

Or are you? Remember that by leaving your career as a big-time attorney you are losing the salary you would have earned there. The implicit cost of owning the bicycle shop is the $50,000 of foregone salary as an attorney. So your economic profit is -$500 (or $62,500 - $13,000 - $50,000). In real, economic terms you are taking a loss! This is not to say that you shouldn't stay in the bicycle shop, because there might be compensating "psychic" benefits from living your childhood dream. The purpose here is to underscore that you should be aware of *all* of the relevant costs of your choices.

Now let's take another look at economic profit. There are two types of economic profit: normal and supernormal.

- A firm makes a **normal profit** if it is making enough to compensate the owner for his or her implicit costs—in other words, if economic profit is zero. Continuing with our bicycle shop example, if your revenues happened to be exactly $63,000 you would be making a normal profit because your revenue would be just enough to cover your explicit costs ($13,000) *and* "pay" yourself enough ($50,000) to make it worth your while not to be a lawyer. The normal profit represents the "normal" return to the owners of the firm for investing their time, energy, and capital in the firm.
- A firm makes **supernormal profit** if its revenues exceed all costs, explicit and implicit—in other words, if economic profit is positive. If your revenue from the bicycle shop were $70,000, for example, you would be making a supernormal profit of $7,000 (or $70,000 - $63,000). In other words you would be making $7,000 more than the minimum amount you would require ($50,000) to stay in business.

Supernormal economic profits play a vital role in the market capitalist economy. The prospect of such profits induces entrepreneurs to undertake risky, innovative projects, which in turn spur long-term economic growth. Furthermore, if one firm enjoys such profits, other firms may try to emulate its success and enter the business. In other words, supernormal profit may act as a signal to encourage firms to put their resources in those sectors that need them most. Paradoxically, supernormal profits may carry the seeds of their own demise. If new firms can enter an industry in response to supernormal profits in that industry, the increased competition may lead to a fall in prices that will ultimately cause profit to fall back its "normal" level.

SHAREHOLDER VALUE

Value maximization (sometimes called **shareholder wealth maximization**) is closely related to profit maximization. Before explaining exactly what this means, we need to make a little detour to explain the concept of discounting.

Compounding, Discounting, and Present Values

An **interest rate** is the price that a borrower has to pay a lender for the use of his or her money. For example, imagine that your little brother wants to buy a car that costs $10,000. He is broke, so he comes to you and asks to borrow the whole sum. You agree to help on condition that in one year he repays the $10,000 (the **principal**) and an extra $300 (the interest). The interest rate you are charging is 3 percent (300 / 10,000).

Now imagine that instead of lending the $10,000 to your brother you put it into a savings account at the bank. The bank pays you an interest rate of 3 percent per year for the use of your money. How much will you have from this investment in one year? The answer is $10,300 or $10,000 \times (1 +.03)$.

Suppose you take this amount and reinvest it again for another year. Now how much will you have? The answer is $10,609 = $10,300 \times (1 + .03) = $10,000 \times (1 + .03)^2$.

If you rolled the investment over for yet another year you would have about $10,927 + $10,000 \times (1 + .03)^2$.

After ten years you would have about $13,347.9 = $10,000 \times (1 + .03)^{10}$. Notice how quickly your investment increases in value. This is the magic of compounding: The interest that you reinvest earns interest itself, which earns even more interest, and so forth. In formulaic terms, compounding means if you invest $1 today at an annual interest rate of r then in n years you will have earned **$1 \times (1 + r)^n$** dollars.

The power of compounding means that if you save even a little when you are young, you should be able to live very comfortably when you retire. In a provocative new book, *Animal Spirits*, Nobel laureate George Akerlof and financial economist Robert Schiller provide a good example of how this works: Imagine a young couple that manages to save $20,000 a year for ten consecutive years while they are in their twenties and early thirties, but then never save a dime for the rest of their lives. If the interest rate on their investment was 7 percent (which is not unreasonable), then at age sixty-five they would have accumulated more than $3 million! So the sooner you start saving the better off you will be.

Other than exhorting you to save, however, our purpose here is to introduce and underscore a fundamental principle: *A dollar today will be worth more than a dollar tomorrow.* An important corollary is that *getting a dollar tomorrow is worth less than getting a dollar today.* To see this more clearly, just ask yourself the following question: If the interest rate is 3 percent, how much would I have to invest in order to get $1 a year from now? The answer is **$1 / (1 + .03)** because investing this amount would yield exactly

$$\$1 = \frac{\$1}{1 + .03} \times (1. + 03)$$

Alternatively, getting $1 next year is worth only $.97 = $1 / (1 + .03) to you today. Similarly, a dollar two years from now is worth only $.94 = $1 / (1 + .03)^2 today, a dollar three years from now is worth only $.91 = $1/ (1 + .03)^2, and so forth. Notice that dollars in the future are **discounted** relative to current dollars. In general, suppose that the interest rate is r. We say that the **discounted present value** of a dollar n years from now is $\$1 / (1 + r)^n$.

If this sounds like a dry academic exercise, consider the following application (inspired by an incident that actually happened in California many years ago). Suppose that you and your friends get together to buy a lottery ticket for a $500,000 prize. You are overjoyed when you win! However, it turns out that you don't get the $100,000 all at once. Instead, the state pays it out in increments of $100,000 over a five year period. Some of you would be happy to divide $100,000 now and then wait for the rest, but most of you would prefer to have the entire lump sum of $500,000 right now. You put an ad in the paper offering to sell your lottery ticket. The idea is that you will sell the right to receive the sequence of five payments of $100,000 each over the next five years in exchange for a cash payment of $500,000 today.

Now suppose that the interest rate is 5 percent. How much would someone be willing to pay to get the right to receive the five $100,000 installment payments? Getting $100,000 next year is worth only $95,000 = $100,000 / (1 + .05) today, and getting $100,000 in two years is worth only $90,000 = $100,000 / (1 + .05)^2 today, and so on up to the fifth year. The discounted present value of the sequence of payments is

$$\$452{,}798 = \$100{,}000 + \frac{\$100{,}000}{1 + .05} + \frac{\$100{,}000}{(1 + .05)^2} + \frac{\$100{,}000}{(1 + .05)^3} + \frac{\$100{,}000}{(1 + .05)^4} + \frac{\$100{,}000}{(1 + .05)^5}$$

So the most you could get by selling your $500,000 lottery ticket is a bit more than $450,000!

The Value of the Firm

By now you are probably wondering what on earth this has to do with shareholder value. The answer is "everything."

Imagine a corporation that pays out its profits every quarter as dividends to its stockholders. Let's denote the dividends today by d_0 (d for dividends, 0 for time today), dividends next quarter by d_1, dividends the quarter after that by d_2, and so on. For simplicity we'll assume that there is no uncertainty, so everyone knows exactly what all the dividends will be. How much would you be willing to pay for a share of this stock? If you buy it, you will receive the sequence of dividends d_0, d_1, d_2 . . . if the interest rate is r, then the discounted present value of this stream of dividends is

$$d_0 \quad + \quad \frac{d_0}{(1+r)} \quad + \quad \frac{d_1}{(1+r)^2} \quad + \quad \frac{d_3}{(1+r)^3} \quad + \quad \text{etc.}$$

This corresponds to the present value calculation for the lottery, except that here the sum keeps on going forever because, as you will recall from Chapter 2, the corporation is an artificial person who never dies. Thus this present value is what the sequence of dividend payments is worth today, so neither you nor anyone else would be willing to pay more than this amount. It follows that the *price* of the share of stock today is exactly

$$\text{Price per share} \quad = \quad d_0 \quad + \quad \frac{d_1}{1+r} \quad + \quad \frac{d_2}{(1+r)^2} \quad + \quad \frac{d_3}{(1+r)^3}$$

This is very important as it clearly shows that *the price of a stock should equal the discounted present value of the future dividends paid out by the firm*. It implies that the stock price measures the current value of the market's expectations about the *future* performance of the firm. The **value of the firm**, or its **shareholder value**, is simply the price per share multiplied by the number of outstanding shares:

$$\text{Value} = \text{Price per Share} \times \text{Number of Shares}$$

Profit Maximization versus Value Maximization

Let us grant the premise that the managers of a firm should try to work in the interests of its owners. Which objective should the managers try to maximize, profit or value? In answering this question there are two distinct criteria to consider: First, which objective best captures the interests of the owners? Second, which objective is the better method of guiding managers to doing their job effectively? Moreover, the objective needs to be clearly defined and measurable. Given these parameters, value maximization beats profit maximization on all counts. There are several specific reasons for this:

- It is not clear how profits should be measured. Quarterly? Yearly? The stock price, however, is a single, readily accessible number that reflects the market's best assessment of how the firm is, and will be, doing.
- It is fairly easy for managers to fudge their reported profits by using a number of accounting tricks. The stock price is set by the market and is not so easily manipulated.
- Profit is at heart a static concept. It measures the performance of the firm only over a given time period. This would be fine if the managers maximized profit every period and the profits in one period did not influence those in other periods. In fact, there are a number of reasons to think that profits today affect profits (and hence dividends) in the future. For example, managers might forego costly investments or avoid expenditures in research and development (R&D) as a way to raise profits today, but at the expense of lowering productivity and profit in the future. Furthermore, the firm may benefit from **learning-by-doing**. This occurs when the more workers apply themselves to particular tasks the more likely they are to come up with good ideas to raise productivity. If so, it may pay to produce more early on as a way to lower current costs and increase profits in the future. There are also examples of firms that deliberately incurred losses initially to make bigger profits in the future.
- Because profits are static, they are not equipped to assess the value of the timing or duration of investments. Is it better to invest in a project that raises profits by $100 million next year, or a project that raises profits by $10 million every year for the next ten years? (Think about our example of the lottery.) The stock price correctly discounts all expected future profits.
- Because profits are static, they are also not equipped to capture the effects of uncertainty about the firm's profits in the future. Investment projects may differ in terms of risk; different firms may be more or less risk prone depending upon the extent to which they rely upon debt or equity to finance their investments. (Firms with lots of debt are said to be highly **leveraged**; the market perceives them as more risky than firms that are less leveraged. More of this in Chapter 7.) It may not be obvious at first glance how stock prices

How to Use a Huge Loss to Make a Huge Profit

A famous case of a firm deliberately incurring a loss to pave the way for huge future profits centers on the legendary Chung Ju Yung, the founder of Hyundai. In 1960 the South Korean government was taking bids to build a bridge in their capital city, Seoul. Mr. Yung supposedly bid 1 Korean won (worth less than 1 cent in US dollars!) to build the bridge, a bid the government of South Korea gleefully accepted. Yung took a big loss but also earned the gratitude of the government and so attracted many profitable government grants later.

deal with this problem either. This is only because we made the simplifying assumption here that all future dividends are known with certainty. In finance classes you will learn fancy ways of incorporating the effects of risk into stock prices. What basically happens is that the price of the stock is still equal to a properly discounted sum of future dividends, but there is a "risk adjustment" tacked on. Investors shy away from riskier firms, so their stock prices tend to be lower than those of less risky firms.

SHAREHOLDERS VERSUS STAKEHOLDERS

What should be the objective of the firm? The traditional view, upon which we have been elaborating at length, is that the managers of the firm should act solely in the interests of its owners. This is expressed in the concrete objective of value maximization. Over the last thirty years, however, this paradigm has come under attack. Critics argue that the firm has moral responsibilities toward a range of constituencies, called **stakeholders**, other than shareholders alone. We'll begin by defining who these stakeholders might be and then discuss how the firm might meet their needs. Then we will return to the debate—a philosophical construct, but one with profound practical importance—over the objectives of shareholder value and stakeholder value.

Who (or What) Are Stakeholders?

Broadly speaking, a stakeholder is anyone or anything that either affects or is affected by the behavior of the firm. This definition is so all-encompassing as to be of little use. H. Jeff Smith, the philosopher who first attracted attention to stakeholder value in the early 1980s, went so far as to include *competitors* as stakeholders. Michael Jensen, the Nobel laureate first mentioned in Chapter 2, facetiously commented that according to this definition " . . . the environment, terrorists, blackmailers, and thieves" should also be considered stakeholders. Suffice it to say that there is an ongoing debate about who exactly should be considered a stakeholder, and there are even methods to determine whom the stakeholders of a particular firm might be. Nonetheless, everyone agrees that a minimal set of stakeholders for any firm would include the following:

Employees, who have an interest in fair pay and safe working conditions.

Suppliers, who have an interest in regular business from the company and prompt payment.

Customers, who have an interest in fair prices and safe products.

The *community*, which has an interest in the jobs provided by the firm, and in general its ability to do business in a way that contributes to the life of the community.

It is easy to add to the list by including things like "the environment," "future generations," "creditors," etc. You get the idea. The firm doesn't exist just to benefit its owners, but to benefit everyone (and everything) touched by its activities.

Look at this list again. Notice that in each case the firm's responsibility to the party in question is already at least partially defined by law. Consider your employees, for example. As an employer you are prohibited from discriminatory hiring and sexual harassment, you have to comply with occupational health and safety regulations, you have to abide by laws governing minimum wages and overtime, and so on. It goes without saying that you have to obey the law. The question is how much *beyond* the law you should go in looking after the interests of your employees. Should you provide educational benefits, for example? Should you provide childcare services? How much job security should you guarantee? Do you have a responsibility to keep a plant open even if it is losing money? These are complicated questions; the business world is filled with difficult ethical dilemmas. The shareholder value and stakeholder value schools of thought will at first glance seem diametrically opposed in their respective approaches to these types of issues. But we will see that, functionally if not philosophically, they arrive at close to the same place.

Let us first consider these two approaches to business in their extreme forms, and then see how they might be reconciled.

Shareholder Maximization

According to the traditional school of thought *the objective of the firm should be to maximize shareholder value*. Aside from the fact that the managers of the firm have a fiduciary responsibility to look after the interests of the stockholders, there is a deep economic argument to justify shareholder maximization. As we have seen, profits serve as signals to attract new resources into sectors where they can be used most efficiently. Stock prices serve a similar function. Firms that offer high returns to their stockholders will attract investors to put their financial capital where it can be used most efficiently. Think of the total value of production in an economy as a "pie." Profit and shareholder maximization help to make this pie as big as possible by providing incentives for resources and financial capital to be allocated in the most efficient way. The paradox is that society is better off—in the sense that the pie is bigger—despite that fact that the owners of the firm are acting selfishly. As Adam Smith famously put it in *The Wealth of Nations* in 1776, the businessman

> . . . by directing that industry in such a manner as its produce may be of the greatest value, he intends only his own gain, and he is in this, as in many other cases, led by an invisible hand to promote an end which was no part of his intention. Nor is it always the worse for the society that it was no part of it. By pursuing his own interest he frequently promotes that of the society more effectually than when he really intends to promote it. I have never known much good done by those who affected to trade for the public good."

Two criticisms have been levied against this view. To begin with, shareholder maximization is often painted as amoral and heartless. Think of Michael Douglas playing Gordon Gekko in the movie *Wall Street*. "Greed," he announces smugly, "is good." This is a caricature as no advocate of shareholder maximization would actually speak in favor of unethical behavior. Even Milton Friedman, the great exponent of free-market capitalism said that the firm should maximize profit, but only " . . . so long as it plays by the rules of the game, which is to say, engages in free and open competition, without deception or fraud." You should also remember that the argument does not suggest that the ethics, social responsibility, and the "public good" do not matter. Instead, paradoxically, it posits that these laudable ends may be best achieved by allowing the owners of firms to pursue their own interests. Interfering with the profit motive would reduce the size of the economic "pie," so that there might actually be less wealth available to expend on the "public good."

A more compelling criticism is that, as an empirical matter, the present-value formula for stock prices that we developed earlier only seems to explain the behavior of stock prices in the "long run." Some economists argue that in the "short run" it does poorly. The problem is this: The return that investors receive from the stock consists both of dividends payments and **capital gains**, the increase in the price of the stock over time. If you buy the stock today at $50 a share and it increases in value to $52, you have made a 4 percent profit, even if you receive no dividends. This means that stock prices can increase just because people expect them to increase: I bet that prices will increase because I expect that you expect that prices will increase, and you expect that I expect that prices will increase because you expect me to expect you to expect prices to increase . . .

This is the essence of a **speculative bubble**. Although it is a contentious issue, the evidence is that over extended periods the "fundamentals" of dividends will dominate and our present-value formula will hold. Over shorter periods, however, these self-fulfilling expectations can cause stock prices to deviate from what "fundamentals" would dictate. This may happen for quite a while. During the dot.com bubble of the 1990s, for example, there were companies that didn't pay dividends at all (and were never expected to!), but which outperformed well-established firms on the stock market for several years. This means that in the short run the value of the firm is not a reliable guide to its performance and is an inadequate objective for its managers.

Stakeholder Maximization

More recently, a competing school of thought has argued that *the objective of the firm should be to look after the interests of all its stakeholders*. The premise here is that ethical behavior should always take priority over self-interest. So an employee, for example, is not just a factor of production to be used as a tool to increase your stock price. He or she is a human being who must be treated with respect and dignity, as an end in itself. This view also has an illustrious parentage, being inspired by the great German philosopher Immanuel Kant. "Always recognize," he wrote, "that human individuals are ends, and do not use them as means to your end." Furthermore, the firm itself is viewed as a grand coalition of all the interested parties, so its objective should be to benefit all of them. By doing so it can foster cooperative behavior among the stakeholders that may unleash synergies that may make everyone better off, including the shareholders.

But stakeholder maximization can also be criticized. Stakeholder advocates are often taken to task for ignoring inescapable trade-offs between different stakeholders. How, for example, can it be possible to pay workers more and simultaneously pay extra dividends? The stakeholder advocates' response to this (as Anne Simpson of the World Bank puts it) is that we should resist "the tyranny of the *or.*" You don't necessarily need to choose between high wages *or* high dividends, for example. If you play your cards right you could have high wages *and* high dividends. Why? Human resources experts tell us that "happy workers are productive workers." If you look after your employees, they may become more content and more productive, and so increase the value of your firm.

Another criticism of stakeholder maximization is that it is just too vague an objective to be of practical use in managing a firm. What exactly does it mean, operationally, to look after everyone's interests? We need, as Michael Jensen says, a way of "keeping score." Something easily observable and measurable, like a stock price.

A Synthesis?

So who is right, the shareholder maximizers or the stakeholder maximizers? Perhaps both. On the one hand, shareholder advocates make some good points: It is true that stock prices offer a readily observable, objective measure of the performance of the firm *in the long run*. Furthermore business is filled with difficult ethical trade-offs in which someone must get hurt. Should you shut down a plant in a small town, eliminating jobs and devastating the local economy but keeping the firm alive? Should you invest in a new technology that reduces greenhouse emissions but that raises your costs and reduces your profits? On the other hand, stakeholder advocates also make some good points. Stock prices are, arguably, unreliable measures of the performance of the firm *in the short run*. Furthermore there may be synergies from getting stakeholders to work together cooperatively that may swamp many apparent trade-offs.

The consensus now is that over the long haul it isn't really possible to sustain a business *without* looking after the interests of stakeholders. A corollary to this is that firms have discovered that "they can do well by doing good." Treating their employees fairly and generously fosters a sense of trust and belonging that raises productivity. Treating their suppliers fairly ensures timely provision of quality inputs. Treating customers fairly and providing a quality product creates a sense of brand loyalty that sustains demand for long periods. Michael Jensen recognizes this when he advocates "enlightened value maximization," adopting the *long run* market value of the firm as an objective, provides a good scorecard for the value of the firm. At the same, however, he recognizes that in the long run "we cannot create value without good relations with customers, employees, financial markets, suppliers, regulators, communities, and the rest." At the end of the day it may be that looking after stakeholders in an intrinsic part of maximizing stakeholder value.

SUMMARY

This chapter examined in great detail alternative definitions of cost and profit and explored the importance of economic profit in a market capitalist economy. The intent here was to extend the notion of profit maximization to the broader and more functional notion of value maximization. Value maximization has it critics and has been challenged by advocates of stakeholder maximization. In the end, however, self-interest ultimately requires a concern for others. Perhaps, in the long run, there can be no value maximization *without* stakeholder maximization.

Further Reading

Akerlof, G., and R. Shiller. *Animal Spirits: How Human Psychology Drives the Economy and Why It Matters for the Global Economy.* Princeton, New Jersey: Princeton University Press, 2009.

Bovée, C., J. Thrall, and M. Mescon. *Excellence in Business.* 3rd ed. Upper Saddle River, N.J.: Pearson, 2007.

Brickley, J., J. Zimmerman, and C. Smith, C. *Managerial Economics & Organizational Architecture.* 5th ed. New York: McGraw-Hill/Irwin, 2008.

Campbell, J., and R. Shiller, R. "Valuation Ratios and the Long-Run Stock Market Outlook." *Journal of Portfolio Management* 24 (1998): 11–26.

Friedman, M. *Capitalism and Freedom.* Chicago: University of Chicago Press, 1962.

Friedman, M. "The Social Responsibility of Business Is to Increase Its Profits." *New York Times Magazine* September 13, 1970: SM17.

Jensen, M. "Value Maximization, Stakeholder Theory, and the Corporate Objective Function." *European Financial Management* 7 (2001): 297–317.

Kant, I. (1797). *Foundations of the Metaphysics of Morals,* translated by Mary Gregor. Cambridge: Cambridge University Press, reprinted 1996.

Mankiw, N.G. *Principles of Economics.* 6th ed. Mason, Ohio: Southwestern Publishing Company, 2012.

Narayanan, M., and V. Nanda. , V. *Finance for Strategic Decision Making: What Non-financial Managers Need to Know.* New York: John Wiley & Sons, 2008.

Simpson, A. Shareholders and Stockholders: the Tyranny of the Or. Asia Corporate Governance Roundtable, 3rd meeting. April 3, 2001.

Vidal, D. Reward Trumps Risk: How Business Perspectives in Corporate Citizenship and Sustainability are Changing. Conference Board Report Q-00216-06-EA, 2006.

CHAPTER 4

THE EXTERNAL ENVIRONMENT

They talk a good game, but economists hardly know enough about business cycles to figure where they come from, let alone where they are going.
—Gary Becker, Nobel laureate in Economics

A strategy delineates a territory in which a company seeks to be unique.
—Michael Porter

So far we have looked at how firms can be organized and what they are trying to do. Now we turn our attention to the economic environment in which they operate. Michael Porter, a Harvard professor who is one of the towering figures in management theory, asserted that the external environment can be broken into two parts, the macro environment and the micro environment.

"Macro" is a Greek word meaning "large," so macroeconomics is the study of the *aggregate* economy in its entirety. It involves things like GDP and inflation and unemployment that you hear about everyday in the news. Our first objective in this chapter is to provide a crash course in macroeconomics, defining what these terms mean, sketching the core concepts of macroeconomic analysis, and discussing how the macro economy impinges upon you as a businessman or businesswoman.

Because "micro" means "small" in Greek you might guess that "microeconomics" deals with economics on a small scale. But what "small" means in practice depends upon the context; for our purposes it means the particular industry in which your firm operates. Our second objective in this chapter is to address the basic question of how the economic environment of the industry affects the profitability of your firm. To address this question we turn to a framework developed by Michael Porter. In 1980, Porter wrote *Competitive Advantage*, an influential book that offered a systematic method for thinking about how an industry "works." This method, called **five-forces analysis**, can be applied both to evaluate the profitability of your firm in a particular industry and to develop ways of improving its competitive advantage.

THE MACRO ENVIRONMENT AND YOUR BUSINESS

This first section has two objectives. First, it will tell you enough about macroeconomics to enable you to understand the macroeconomic news in the popular press and in the news. Second, it will alert you to how changes in the macroeconomy can impact you, your firm, and your industry.

Macroeconomic Things

The important thing to remember is that macroeconomics deals with the behavior of the entire economy. Macroeconomists are not concerned with why unemployment is high in Cleveland or real-estate prices are low in Iowa. Instead they are concerned with unemployment and real estate prices nationwide. So the first thing we need to do is define some of the key measures of aggregate economic activity.

Aggregate Production

What does aggregate production mean? If your firm produces bicycles, it is easy enough to measure your production: It is just the number of bikes you make. But what if our economy makes two goods, bicycles and Lady GaGa CDs? These two things are incommensurate (we can't just add them up), so how can we measure aggregate production? The answer is that we need a common "yardstick" against which we can measure both goods. That yardstick is the dollar (or the Yuan, or the euro). To see how this works, consider the following example.

Table 4.1 reports the quantity of bikes and CDs produced in two different years, 2010 and 2015. Ignore the year 2015 for a moment. The total value in dollars of all the goods produced in the economy in 2010 is $17,250 = ($1,500 × 10) + ($15 × 150). So aggregate production measured in dollars in 2010 is $17,250. This leads to our first definition: **Nominal Gross Domestic Product** (known affectionately as "GDP" to economists) is the total value of all currently produced, final goods and services traded in markets in an economy over a given time period.

Because you will hear the term GDP bandied about a lot, it is important to understand exactly what it means, what it includes and what it doesn't. "Nominal" means that it is measured in dollars. "Currently produced" means that used

TABLE 4.1
Aggregate Production: Bikes and CDs

	Quantity of Bikes	Price of a Bike	Quantity of CDs	Price of a CD
2010	10	$1500	150	$15
2015	12	$1600	200	$12

goods are not counted in GDP (for example, a used car doesn't count). "Final" means that it does not include intermediate goods, things used to produce other things (so bread is included, but not the flour used to make it). "Traded in markets" means that it does not include things like the time you spend cleaning your house or cooking dinner (although hiring a maid and going to a restaurant would count). So in our bicycle and CD example, nominal GDP in 2010 is $17,750. As an exercise see if you can calculate nominal GDP in 2015 by using the same formula we applied to 2010.

Nominal GDP can change for two reasons, either because actual production of the goods changes, or because the prices of the goods change. For this reason it is often important to adjust the measurement of GDP in a way that allows us to abstract from price changes. To do this, we define **real GDP** as current production assuming that prices have not changed from a previous period (called the base period). So using our bicycle/CD example, if 2015 is the current year and 2010 is the base year, then real GDP in 2015 is $21,000 = ($1,500 x 12) + ($15 x 200). Notice that real GDP has increased by less than nominal GDP in this example. Real GDP per capita (that is, per person) is often used as a measure of the standard of living. (Actually, real GDP is no longer calculated with prices from a base year. Instead, it is calculated with "chain-weighted" prices from the previous two years. But this is a technicality.)

Another important macroeconomic concept is **national income**. Your income is the money you get from your salary and from whatever assets you own. The same idea (albeit on a much greater scale) applies to the whole economy. Way back in Chapter 1, you read that there are four basic factors of production: land, labor, capital, and entrepreneurship. So national income consists of *the total payments to all of the factors of production in the economy* (rent, wages and salaries, interest, and profit). If you think about it for a moment, you will see that *every dollar of stuff produced in the economy (which is GDP) must generate a dollar of income for somebody (which is income)*. Ignoring for the moment some fine points that need not concern us here, this essentially means that we can use

"GDP" and "income" as synonyms (the triple equality sign in the equation that represents this concept means "true by definition"):

$$GDP \equiv Income$$

Who buys all the stuff that is produced in GDP? To answer this question we need to define a few more terms:

- **Consumption** consists of all the goods and services purchased by households. Consumption represents about 70 percent of GDP.
- **Investment** consists of purchases of new capital by firms. It also includes new residential construction by households and inventory accumulation or decumulation by firms. If a firm can't sell everything it has produced, it puts what has not been sold in inventory; these items are considered an investment because the firm can presumably sell them in the future.
- **Government expenditures** are the goods and services purchased by the government.
- **Exports** are the goods and services that we sell to foreign countries.
- **Imports** are the goods and services that we buy from foreign countries.
- **The trade balance** is the difference between what we export and what we import.

These component parts are related to GDP as follows:

$$GDP \equiv Consumption + Investment + Government\ Expenditures + Exports - Imports$$

What this means is that the total value of what we produce (GDP, or income) must equal **aggregate expenditures**, the total value of what is consumed by households, firms, the government, and foreign countries. The reason we subtract imports to arrive at aggregate expenditure is because "consumption" is total expenditure on *all* goods, domestic and foreign, so total expenditure on domestic goods by domestic consumers is considered "consumption–imports."

Aggregate Prices

In the numerical example shown in Table 4.1 you may have noticed that although the price of bikes went up between 2010 and 2015, the price of Lady GaGa CDs went down (OK, I'm expressing my own musical tastes). At the macro level, however, we have to ask whether prices *on average* have gone up or down. To answer this question we calculate **price indices**, which are nothing more than weighted averages of individual prices. There are many price indices, but the one you are probably most familiar with is the **Consumer Price Index** or CPI. To calculate CPI the government defines a basket of goods and services that it thinks a normal suburban family would consume. Then, once a month, it sends out bureaucrats to check on all of the prices of all of the goods in this hypothetical basket. If the price of the basket has gone up, we can say that prices on average have increased.

Let's analyze this in terms of our little two-good economy. In 2010 the government sees that the "basket" of goods purchased by consumers consists of 10 bikes and 150 CDs. The prices of bikes and CDs were $1,500 and $15 respectively, so the cost of this bundle in 2010 was $17,250 = ($1500 × 10) + ($15 × 150). In 2015, however, the prices of bikes and CDs have changed to $1,600 and $12. The *same* (2010) bundle of 10 bikes and 150 CDs now costs $17,800 = ($1600 × 10) + ($12 × 150). We can conclude that on average prices have increased by about 3 percent [.03 = ($17,800 − $17,250) / $17,250]. The **inflation rate** is defined as the percentage change in the price level, so our inflation rate in this example is 3 percent.

Employment and Unemployment

The **labor force** consists of everybody who has a job or who is looking for one but can't find one. **Employment** is defined as the number of people who have jobs. **Unemployment** is the number of people who are willing and able to take a job, but who can't find one. In other words, unemployment = labor force - employment. In the press you hear about the **unemployment rate** almost every day. It is defined as the ratio of unemployment to the labor force, or

$$\text{unemployment rate} = \frac{\text{labor force} - \text{employment}}{\text{labor force}}$$

This needs to be interpreted with care. For example, not so long ago the government announced that the unemployment rate had declined. Certain politicians took this as a sign that the economy was recovering from the financial crisis. However, at the same time that the unemployment rate was falling, employment was declining. This was interpreted to mean that the unemployment rate was not increasing because things were getting better. But what was really happening was that the unemployment rate was decreasing because some people were so discouraged that they had stopped looking for jobs and had dropped out of the labor force!

Exchange Rates

An **exchange rate** is simply the price of one currency in terms of another. For example, suppose that our domestic currency is the dollar and Germany's foreign currency is the euro. Then the exchange rate is the price of the euro in terms of dollars, that is, how many dollars have to be sacrificed to buy one euro (sometimes it is expressed in reverse as the price of a dollar in terms of euros). The exchange rate is important because it affects the relative price of goods and services in different countries. Suppose, for example, that I am planning to buy a fine pair of Italian shoes when I visit Europe next year. The shoes cost 100 euros and, for simplicity, let's say the exchange rate is $1. Then I expect to spend $100 for my shoes. But suppose that that the euro **appreciates** (it increases in value; when the value of a currency decreases it is said to **depreciate**) to $1.5. How much will my shoes cost me now? For each euro I will have to give up $1.5, rather than $1.0, so the price of my shoes in dollars has increased to $150. This may be enough to dissuade me from buying them.

Fundamental Facts About Macroeconomics

Figure 4.1 shows GDP since 1940. Glancing at this graph reveals two important facts that can be viewed as a positive and a negative trend.

The good news is that over the long term GDP has grown over time, at an average rate of about 3 percent per year. The dotted curve in the graph depicts this long-run trend of growth in the economy. Why should we care about the

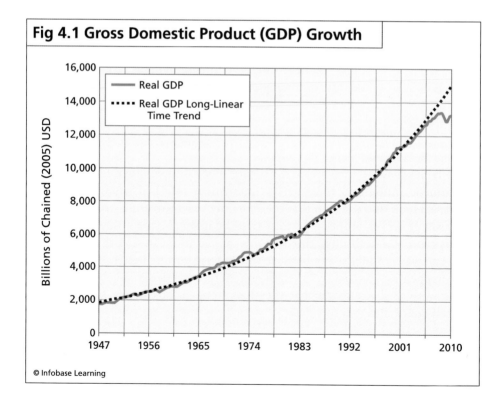

Fig 4.1 Gross Domestic Product (GDP) Growth

Real GDP

Real GDP Long-Linear Time Trend

Billions of Chained (2005) USD

© Infobase Learning

steady growth in GDP? Recall from Chapter 3 that, because of the miracle of compounding, small changes in the interest rate can cause very large changes in your wealth over time. Likewise, small increases in the growth rate of GDP over extended periods can cause very large increases in income. The long term growth rate is a key ingredient in our economic health and standard of living.

The bad news is that there have been substantial fluctuations in this trend. These fluctuations constitute what is popularly called the **business cycle**. Periods when GDP is increasing are called **expansions**, whereas periods when GDP is falling are called **contractions**. A **recession** was traditionally defined as occurring when GDP fell for at least two quarters. Because this is rather arbitrary, however, a recession is now announced by a committee of wise men at the National Bureau of Economic Research (NBER) who study the state of the economy.

Why should we care about the business cycle? A fall in GDP (a recession) causes income to decrease, so that the economic "pie" shrinks. Furthermore, as the economy contracts, workers are laid off so that employment falls and unemployment increases. Look again at Figure 4.1. Notice the recessions in 1974, 1979, 1981, 2001, and the Great Recession after 2008. Then look at the sustained period without serious downturns from 1981 until 2001, part of the Great Moderation first mentioned in Chapter 1.

Figure 4.2 plots data on the CPI over the same period and also yields two important facts. The first is that there has been a sustained increase in prices since the Second World War. The second is that prices increased most rapidly from the late 1960s until 1981—a period called the Great Inflation. After that, they grew less quickly, from the Great Moderation of the 1980s and 1990s up until today. Since then inflation has been tamed, but keep your fingers crossed because the business cycle has a tendency to change things.

A related question is why we should care about inflation. This is a deep question with no single right answer. One answer is that people have to spend time and money keeping track of price changes. This means we waste some of what we produce on watching prices rather than using it on something useful. Another answer is that inflation can redistribute wealth from lenders to borrowers. Suppose you pay a fixed interest rate of 3 percent on your mortgage, for example. Imagine that inflation takes off to 4 percent. The bank earns 3 percent from your mortgage payment, but every dollar it gets from you is worth 4 percent less because of the inflation. Its *real* rate of return is *minus* one percent. It is as though the bank is paying you to have a mortgage! This actually happened during the Great Inflation, from the late 1960s through the 1970s, a situation that made many homeowners quite happy and many banks very nervous.

Fig 4.2 Consumer Price Index (CPI) All Items

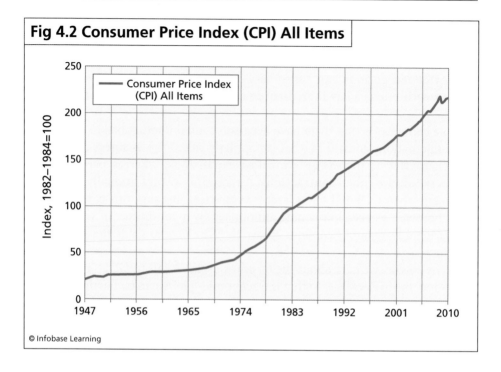

© Infobase Learning

Fundamental Concepts of Macroeconomics

There are two basic macroeconomic questions. The first asks "What causes countries to enjoy sustained growth and what policies the government can implement to encourage it?" The short answer is that long-run growth in GDP ultimately depends upon fundamental things like capital accumulation and technological growth; policies that encourage investment, education, and research and development may stimulate growth. The other question is "What causes business cycles, and what can the government do about them?" We will focus on this question here, because it concerns a subject heavily covered by the press these days and is something that will most immediately impinge upon your business. Let's begin by revisiting the GDP identity first introduced in the discussion of aggregate production and aggregate expenditure:

$$\text{GDP} \equiv \text{Consumption} + \text{Investment} + \text{Government Expenditures} + \text{Exports} - \text{Imports}$$

A good place to start is to notice that an increase or decrease in the left-hand side of the equation (GDP) must be associated with a corresponding increase or decrease in the right-hand side (aggregate expenditure). A concrete example may be helpful here, so let's think about the downturn in the economy after 2008, something we now call the Great Recession. What caused it? The fault cannot be attributed to a single event or a single player; what really caused it was a sequence of actions by various players. The financial crisis that began in 2008 effectively "froze" the financial markets. Suddenly banks stopped making loans. Households responded by reducing consumption expenditures; likewise, firms cut back their investment expenditures. This made demand for goods and services fall (the right-hand side of the equation), so firms were forced to reduce production and lay off workers. Hence we had a fall in GDP (the left-hand side). This in turn reduced consumers' income, so that they spent even less, making GDP fall even more, which made consumption fall more, and so on.

Financial Turmoil → Consumption ↓ and Investment ↓ → Aggregate Expenditure ↓ → GDP ↓

Hence the Great Recession: GDP fell, employment fell, and unemployment increased. How did the government respond to the crisis? First, it took a number of measures, unprecedented in kind or scope, to "unfreeze" the financial markets by offering financial assistance to large banks and financial institutions, buying up many of the "toxic" assets that had caused the crisis. This was intended to improve confidence in the financial markets, in the hope that consumption and investment would rebound. However, the government also turned to its two conventional policy tools for managing the business cycle: monetary policy and fiscal policy.

Monetary Policy

Monetary policy is the manipulation of the money supply and interest rates. "Money" is what we use to pay for transactions. The basic definition of "money" used by the government (there are several broader definitions) is called M1. It consists of currency (the cash in your pocket) and demand deposits (checking accounts) because most transactions are consummated using one of these two means. The **Federal Reserve**, often just called **the Fed**, is our **central bank**, the institution responsible for controlling our money supply. The traditional philosophy as to how this affects economic activity is that monetary policy works through interest rates: Suppose that the Fed observes a decline in GDP. If it increases the money supply, there will be more money available to lend out, so interests rates will fall. As interest rates fall, firms have to pay less to borrow, so they invest more. The increase in investment raises aggregate expenditure, which raises GDP.

Money ↑ → Interest Rates ↑ → Aggregate Expenditures ↑ → GDP ↑

During the Great Recession, however, the Fed cut interest rates so much that they were effectively zero. This limited the power of monetary policy—at least as traditionally understood—to stimulate the economy, because interest rates can't fall below zero.

Fiscal Policy

Fiscal policy is the manipulation of taxes and government expenditures. At the Federal level fiscal policy is established jointly by the executive branch (the President) and the legislative branch (Congress). To combat the Great Recession the government implemented a stimulus package that raised government expenditures:

Government Expenditures ↑ → Aggregate Expenditures ↑ → GDP ↑

There was heated debate about whether it would have been better to cut taxes rather than raise government expenditures. A tax cut would have stimulated the economy by raising consumption:

Taxes ↓ → Consumption ↑ → Aggregate Expenditures ↑ → GDP ↑

The problem now is that to finance the increased expenditures the government has had to borrow more. This contributes to an already large public debt. At some point we will have to reduce government expenditures or raise taxes or both. But this in turn means that, in order to prevent aggregate expenditures from decreasing, something else must increase. Consumption is unlikely to increase much, because too many households are already heavily indebted. This leaves only one alternative, namely an increase in exports. And in fact, exporting industries have been the only part of the economy doing well during the recession.

You and the Business Cycle

How does the business cycle affect your business, and how should you respond to it? The first step in answering this question is to develop a feel for how sensitive the demand for your product is to fluctuations in aggregate economic activity. Some industries are largely unaffected by the business cycle. Dairy farmers, for example, are fairly insulated from the cycle because consumption of milk doesn't change much when incomes change. Other industries, like tourism and restaurants, are very sensitive to the cycle, particularly to changes in income. It is common to see small restaurants go out of business during a recession. On the other hand, it is sometimes surprising to discover which goods are sensitive to the business cycle. One might think, for example, that the demand for toilet paper would be fairly stable over the cycle. In fact, it seems that as the economy expands people shift dramatically up from one-ply, to two-ply, to three-ply rolls. In fact, there are business forecasters who track the demand for toilet paper as a way of measuring consumer confidence!

Every firm, however, will be impacted by business fluctuations, so it is essential to have a strategy in place to deal with upturns and downturns. In a downturn you should plan to lay off workers and curtail purchases from suppliers. Your Human Resource Department might encourage older workers to retire by offering early retirement packages. You should reduce your inventories in anticipation of lower sales. At the same time, though, you might try to mitigate the fall in demand by lowering prices or by running an aggressive marketing campaign. You should reduce capital investments.

Things go in reverse during the upturn. Now you will hire new workers and lock into favorable contracts with suppliers. In fact, if you are proactive, this might be a good time to acquire some really good employees: If you act soon enough you might be able to hire the best and the brightest at low salaries before your competitors can get at them. You should stockpile inventories in expectation of increasing sales. You might consider raising prices. Finally, it would be a good time to undertake capital investments to see you through the boom. Again, if you are proactive, you might time your investments for the bottom of the cycle, just before things take off and when interest rates are still very low.

THE MICRO ENVIRONMENT AND FIVE-FORCE ANALYSIS

Now let's change our focus from the whole economy to a specific industry. Suppose you are thinking about going into business. To assess the potential profitability of your firm you will need to think carefully about how the industry in which you will be operating works. What are the threats and the opportunities to your firm from the economic structure of the industry? Economist Michael Porter developed a simple but powerful way of thinking about this question. It is called **five-force analysis**, because it maps out the way your firm's **competitive advantage** in the industry is affected by the interaction of five fundamental economic forces. The method is still used by consultants when they begin to evaluate the profitability of a new firm or product. However, it also is useful in directing the strategy of an existing firm that is trying to improve its competitive advantage relative to other firms. The five factors are often depicted with a chart like the one presented in Figure 4.3.

Rivalry is the degree to which firms in the industry fight over the market. This is probably the single most important factor in determining profitability and is usually placed in the center of the chart because of its central importance and because it is influenced by the other four. Because of this, we will explore the other four factors first, leaving rivalry for last.

Barriers to Entry

Your firm may be threatened not only by existing firms in the industry, but also by potential entrants to the industry. The more easily you can keep them out,

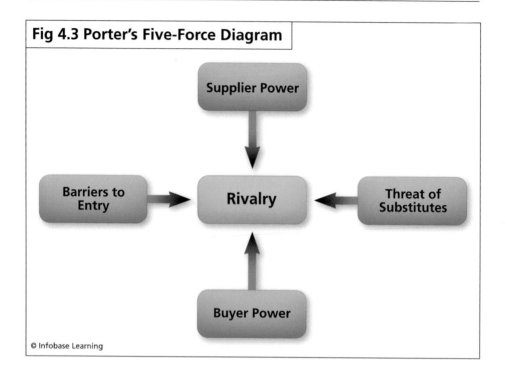

Fig 4.3 Porter's Five-Force Diagram

Supplier Power

Barriers to Entry → Rivalry ← Threat of Substitutes

Buyer Power

© Infobase Learning

the better off you are. **Barriers to entry** are things that make it difficult for other firms to enter. Here are some examples:

- Some barriers to entry are created by the government. For example, local governments normally grant **monopoly** rights to public utilities or cable companies. Small towns often used to grant monopoly rights to a single taxi company or a single ambulance provider. In such cases, there is an insurmountable legal barrier that keeps everyone else out.
- Patents and copyrights constitute particularly important forms of monopoly created by the government. A patent grants exclusive rights to the use of a new invention. However, patents expire after twenty years, so the monopoly power in this case is of only limited duration. Similarly, a copyright effectively grants monopoly rights to proceeds of the publication of a book.
- **Specific assets** are also an effective barrier to entry. You may recall from Chapter 2 that specific assets are assets that can be used only for one purpose. We used the example of the sprocket producer who used a machine that could produce sprockets but nothing else. Specific assets discourage entry for two reasons. On the one

hand, an existing firm (an **incumbent**) has these assets in place and can readily increase production if an entrant challenges it. On the other hand, a potential entrant may be reluctant to spend lots of money that cannot be recouped (sunk costs) if it is forced to leave the industry.

Buyer Power

Moving counterclockwise in the five-force diagram, we find buyer power, which is the ability of a customer to negotiate lower prices. An extreme example of an entity wielding buyer power is the Department of Defense (DOD), which sets the price paid to contractors who provide military hardware to the government. In this case there is only *one* buyer, the Department of Defense, which leaves the contractors very much at the mercy of the DOD decisions on pricing. Less dramatic examples are easy to think of: Wal-Mart, for example, is such a large buyer of appliances that it can negotiate lower prices from manufacturing companies. At the opposite extreme are the people who purchase most consumer products. There are so many consumers, and they are so poorly organized, that none individually has the ability to influence price at all.

Supplier Power

Supplier power is the ability of the firm's suppliers to negotiate higher prices. Suppliers will have more power if they are small in number because the firm has few (or in some case no) alternatives. A good example is large pharmaceutical firms that supply hospitals. Suppliers will also be powerful if it is very costly to switch from one supplier to another. A university that has a contract with Microsoft, for example, might really prefer Apple, but the cost of switching from one to the other would be prohibitive. Conversely, suppliers will be weak if

Brand Loyalty

- An interesting kind of specific asset is **brand loyalty**. Once a firm has earned the loyalty of its customers, it may be hard for new firms to wean them away. For example, some people just prefer to drive Fords, period.

- **Economies of scale**, introduced in Chapter 2, are a classic barrier to entry. Economies of scale occur when per unit costs of production fall the more the firm produces. A large incumbent firm can produce so much that its per unit costs are very low. A small potential entrant can't hope to achieve the same scale of operations and hence will have prohibitively high per unit costs.

there are many of them. An individual wheat farmer would have little leverage against General Foods, for example.

Threat of Substitutes

This factor is often overlooked. It deals with the relationship between the good or service produced in one industry with those produced in other industries. If there are readily available substitutes for the good that you sell, then it is difficult to raise your prices. For example, if Amazon and Apple raise the prices of the Kindle and the iPad—instead of having a price war—people might just start to read old-fashioned books again.

Rivalry

The single most important of the five forces in determining a firm's profitability is **competitive rivalry**. We have this saved for last because the other four feed into it. Rivalry is the struggle between firms for competitive advantage. It is sometimes rated in an ascending scale, starting from "weak" and moving up to "moderate," "intense," and finally "cutthroat." The greater the degree of rivalry the harder it is to gain an advantage over competitors and the harder it is to make profits. The degree of rivalry is influenced by many things, some of which have already been explained in the discussions related to the other four forces:

- Rivalry increases with the number of firms in the industry. As the number of firms increases it becomes harder for any individual firm to influence prices.
- Rivalry becomes more intense when there are high fixed costs (remember these from Chapter 3?). To cover these costs each firm must sell a large quantity, resulting in a struggle for market share.
- Rivalry will be greater when it is difficult for firms to engage in **product differentiation**. If you can't make your product seem different from those of your competitors it will be hard to charge prices greater than theirs. This is why brand loyalty is such a vital asset.
- A contracting economy may reduce demand for the good, causing the market to shrink. Firms are left to squabble over the shrinking pie.
- Rivalry will be weaker when there are strong barriers to entry.
- Specific assets may reduce rivalry by making it hard for potential competitors to enter the industry. However, they may also perversely raise the costs of exiting the industry. If you can't use a machine anywhere but in this industry it makes it costly for you to leave if you are doing badly. Firms reluctant to exit for this reason are left to fight for market share.

An Example of Five-Force Analysis at Work

The best way to see how five-force analysis works is to think through an example in which each of the factors can be applied. Let's return to the bicycle company that was introduced in Chapters 2 and revisited in Chapter 3. We'll lay the groundwork here by resurrecting the scenario used in Chapter 3. Once again, you are a successful lawyer. You have had a life-long dream of making fine bicycles and are tempted to leave the hassles of the courtroom to open your own bicycle company. It would be a fairly small operation producing expensive, upscale bikes. Being prudent, you decide to assess the threats and opportunities of going into business by applying Porter's five-force method to your specific case. What strategies can you implement to ensure profitability? What are the biggest threats to your survival? So get a piece of paper and work though each of the five factors:

1. **Barriers to entry**. It doesn't cost much for a small bicycle producer to set up shop. On the other hand, big producers like Schwinn or Giant enjoy huge economies of scale so you can't hope to compete on price. Does this constitute an effective barrier to entry? Not if you can effectively product differentiate, marketing yourself as a producer of high-quality, hand-made bicycles: the BMW of bikes. You can then compete on the basis of quality, rather than price, by developing a niche market. Furthermore, if you can develop brand loyalty, you would develop your own effective barrier to entry against potential rivals.

2. **Buyer power**. Individual customers are unlikely to have much bargaining power. However, there will be many close substitutes available for your bikes, so you will have limited ability, at least initially, to charge prices higher than other specialty bike companies charge. Furthermore, there is a chance that you could land a contract to provide mountain bikes to the city's new Police Bicycle Squad. This would be such a large contract that you would have to negotiate it with the City Council. In this case there would be substantial buyer power.

3. **Supplier power**. Most of your parts can be purchased in bulk from competitive markets, so overall supplier power is weak. However, you may recall from Chapter 2 that you need a special kind of sprocket. It can only be produced with a special sprocket machine, made to order for you by a single company. The **switching costs** for finding another source would be high, so the sprocket maker has a degree of supplier power that he can use to extort high sprocket prices from you. Conversely, because the sprocket maker has invested a **specific asset**, good for nothing but producing your sprockets, you have a degree of

countervailing negotiating power. As we suggested in Chapter 2, it may be quite expedient for both of you to consider a **vertical merger**, which would provide security to both parties.

4. **Threat of substitutes.** In Europe bicycles are often used to get to work, so public transport is a close substitute. In the United States, however, bicycles are usually used for recreational purposes, so there isn't much in the way of substitutes.

5. **Rivalry.** The bicycle industry is characterized by a few large companies (95 percent of the bikes in the United States are made by large firms based in China or Taiwan) and a fairly large number of smaller producers. You are targeting a niche-market in high quality bikes, however, so there is likely to be heavy competition from other small, upper-end producers.

What does this algorithm tell you? First, you can't expect to compete on price with large companies. Second, there will be spirited competition from other specialty producers. For both reasons it will be essential to differentiate your bikes both from those of large companies and from those of specialty producers. This will require that you not only produce well-engineered, finely crafted bikes, but that you market them aggressively so that you can earn a reputation for quality and establish some brand loyalty. Third, there is little threat from buyer power, unless the city negotiates very low prices for its police bikes. However, the volume of the contract is so large that it is more opportunity than risk. Fourth, supplier power is also likely to be weak. The only possible exception would be the sprocket producer, but that problem can be dealt with neatly by a vertical merger. There is no real threat from substitutes.

Do you decide to go into business? It all depends. It depends upon how much you love the business. It depends upon the implicit costs of the hefty salary you will be giving up. It depends on whether you think you can effectively implement the strategies suggested by the Porter method. The point is that you have logically and systematically appraised the situation and come to have a better understanding of the job ahead of you.

SUMMARY

This chapter surveyed the macro and micro environments that impinge upon your business. It also provided fundamental tools for understanding what you read in the press about macroeconomic events and how they might affect you. It also introduced an algorithm—Porter's famous five-factor analysis—that will enable you to think systematically about how the structure of your industry will affect your profitability and your business strategy. This sets the stage for the next part of the book, which deals with how you can become an entrepreneur and start your own business.

Further Reading

Akerlof, G., and R. Shiller. *Animal Spirits: How Human Psychology Drives the Economy and Why It Matters for the Global Economy.* Princeton, New Jersey: Princeton University Press, 2009.

Mankiw, N.G. *Principles of Economics.* 5th ed. Southwestern Publishing Company, 2008.

Porter, M. *Competitive Strategy.* New York: Free Press, 1980.

———. "How Competitive Forces Shape Strategy." *Harvard Business Review* March/April, 1979.

CHAPTER 5

BECOMING AN ENTREPRENEUR

A creative economy is the fuel of magnificence.
—Ralph Waldo Emerson

We did it (Disneyland), in the knowledge that most of the people
I talked to thought it would be a financial disaster—
closed or forgotten within the first year.
—Walt Disney

Do you dream of going into business for yourself? If so, you are not alone. According to a poll by Junior Achievement in 2009, fully 51 percent of teenagers would like to start their own business someday. The figure has declined a bit—it used to be over 60 percent—because economic times are still hard, but it is high enough to suggest that Americans are endowed with a natural entrepreneurial spirit. So far in this book we have concentrated on the broad sweep and structure of American business, with intimations of how it all might affect your business. Now we get down to brass tacks. In the next three chapters we will discuss concretely what is involved in becoming an entrepreneur. In Chapter 5 we begin with the fundamental question of what you should consider in choosing this path in life. We then move on to the more practical question of how to assess the demand for the good or service you want to provide. You have a great idea, but how will it be received in the marketplace? Assuming that you have had an encouraging answer to this question, Chapter 6 will discuss the nuts and bolts of starting a new company. Assuming that you have flourished, Chapter 7 then discusses how you would go about expanding.

THINGS TO CONSIDER

This section addresses the overarching question: "Do I want to become an entrepreneur?" We begin by providing some basic facts bearing upon this question and a systematic way of approaching it.

Small Business in the United States

Most firms naturally start small, so we will begin by providing some basic facts about small business in the United States. This will give you some idea about the exciting, albeit risky, world you may be entering. Here are some facts about small business in the United States, provided by the U.S. **Small Business Administration (SBA)** Office of Advocacy. The official definition of a "small" firm is that it is independently owned and employs fewer than 500 workers.

- In 2009 there were 27.5 million businesses in the United States. The most recent U.S. Census data revealed that in 2007 there were only 18,311 "large" firms. This meant that 99.9 percent of all businesses were small. In 2008, 21.4 million firms had no employees at all and the remaining 6 million or so had fewer than 500.
- Small businesses employ just over half of the private labor force and produce more than one-half of our GDP.
- 65 percent of the new jobs created between 1993 and 2009 came from small businesses.

These measures of the magnitude of the small business sector do not capture another essential fact: Small businesses are a primary source of technological innovation in our economy. Consider these additional, telling facts, also courtesy of the SBA:

- Small businesses employ 43 percent of the high-tech workers (engineers and scientists) in the economy.
- Small businesses produce 13 times as many patents per employee as large firms do.

This sounds like a wonderfully exciting world, a world where capitalism unleashes the creative potential of people to propel growth and innovation. And it is. But one should always remember that capitalism has two faces: Although the creative and lucky may be rewarded handsomely for their endeavors, the less creative and the unlucky may be weeded out. As the great economist Joseph Schumpeter put it in a now-famous phrase, the capitalist economy grows through a process of **creative destruction**. Strong firms flourish, but weaker firms are purged from the system. To make this more concrete, consider the survival rates of new businesses:

- Seven out of ten new firms are still in business after two years.
- About half of new firms are still in business after five years.
- One-third of these firms last at least 10 years.
- One-quarter stay in business fifteen years or more.

Of course going out of business is not always a bad thing. Some firms *plan* to exist for a short time. These **quick-flip** start-ups typically come up with a technological innovation that they hope to sell to a larger company. The company Divvyshot mentioned in Chapter 2 would seem to be a good example. When its owners sold out to Facebook, they presumably accomplished their objective.

We conclude this overview by mentioning several factors that are changing the face of small business. These are factors that may affect your interest in starting your own business.

E-commerce and the Internet are changing many facets of business. The costs of going into e-commerce are very low. You can work from home, so there is little investment. Wage costs are low since most transactions are consummated electronically. The main costs are to maintain a Website (estimated to be about $600 per month) and possibly a warehouse. Furthermore, there are substantial advantages to e-commerce. You can serve a global market. You can offer great customer service, because the computer can recognize and greet repeat customers. Last but not least, you can set your own hours. These features of e-commerce have led many people to set up shop in their own homes. In fact, one of the most important trends in small business is the growth of **lifestyle companies**. These are companies whose owners have no dreams of being the next Bill Gates, but who go into business hoping to achieve a certain lifestyle and some financial stability for their families.

Another trend is the increased activity of minorities and women in small business. The proportion of businesses owned by minorities increased from 6.8 percent in 1982 to 18 percent in 2002. Among minority-owned firms, those owned by African Americans have seen the highest growth, increasing by an astonishing 45.4 percent between 1997 and 2002. Similarly, the proportion of businesses owned by women increased by 19.8 percent between 1997 and 2002. Women in fact owned 28.2 percent of all the businesses in the country in 2002.

With the introduction of the internet, with a website even a small business can reach millions of potential customers over any distance. *(Shutterstock)*

Another important trend, one that may speak to you personally, is the increased role of young people in small business. Something like 70 percent of all new firms are owned by members of Generation X, people born between 1965 and 1980.

Finally, **downsizing** and **outsourcing** by large firms have had a spill-over effect on small business. When smart, ambitious men and women with lots of human capital got laid off by big employers, they often either went into business for themselves or went to work for someone who was setting up a small business. This fueled innovation in the small business sector by shifting a lot of skilled labor into new businesses.

Advantages and Disadvantages of Going into Business for Yourself

The prospect of opening your own business can be alluring. However, it is important to approach this decision in a systematic way. To provide some structure to your musings on this subject we provide a brief discussion of the advantages and disadvantages of setting your own business. There are a number of attractions to starting up a business:

- It offers the freedom of exercising your *creativity*. There are no pre-set methods or rules or answers, as there would be if, instead of opening your own business, you were to buy into a **franchise**.
- It gives you *independence*. You are your own boss. You make all of the decisions, from what to produce, to how you produce it, how to market it, how to finance it, and where you are located. This can be exhilarating.
- *Start-up costs are low.* It doesn't usually take much capital to get started, and there are many small-business grants (more about this in the next chapter) available. Of course the costs depend upon the structure you adopt (incorporation can be costly, as we saw in Chapter 2). Book-keeping costs are typically low because you can do most of the accounting work yourself on a PC.

Unfortunately there are also a number of disadvantages to starting your own business:

- It gives you *independence*. You are your own boss. You make all of the decisions, from what to produce, to how you produce it, how to market it, how to finance it, and where you are located. The flipside of independence is enormous responsibility.
- It requires a huge commitment of *time* and energy. You may work much longer hours than you would for any other employer.
- It may be *stressful*, with many sleepless nights.
- It is very *risky*. As we saw before, only half of new firms survive five years.
- Without an established presence in the industry it may be difficult to find suppliers who are willing commit to you.
- Similarly, without an established presence it may be hard to woo customers from competing firms until you have established brand loyalty.
- Most new businesses don't make money for the first few years. This **delayed profitability** means that you must expect setbacks; it also means that you will need a financial cushion until things get better. You may have tight budgets with which to finance operations, so good strategy and planning will be vital.
- Finally, to the extent that you do need to acquire capital, it may be hard to find **credit**.

IS THIS FOR ME?

Before choosing to go into business you need to take stock of yourself and ask some hard questions. Do I really have the aptitude and ability to be an entrepreneur? Am I willing to make the necessary sacrifices? To help you ruminate on these questions we will begin—just for fun—with a short quiz that will give you some idea of your "entrepreneurial quotient."

Here is how to score the quiz. The "correct" answer for being a promising entrepreneur is yes (Y) for every question. So add up the number of Ys and then divide by twenty. This gives your entrepreneurial "purity" index. If your purity index is zero, you aren't suited to be an entrepreneur. If your "purity" index is 50 percent you have the potential to be entrepreneur. If your "purity" index is 95 percent you could be the next Richard Branson.

Attributes of Successful Entrepreneurs

Researchers have spent a lot of time trying to identify what makes an entrepreneur. Here are some of the factors that crop up again and again these studies. You may have already guessed what some of them are from the quiz.

- Entrepreneurs are *passionate* about what they do. They are committed to their dream and work tenaciously to accomplish it.
- Entrepreneurs seem to be physically *healthy*. They have the energy and stamina to put in long hours for extended periods.
- Entrepreneurs tend to be *smart* and *eager to learn*. They have superior analytical skills and are voracious about acquiring new information that may be useful to them.
- Entrepreneurs have what psychologists call a strong **locus of control**. This means that they believe that they can control the external events impacting them. In fact, they have the need to control and direct the things around them. This may be why they may be drawn to self-employment.
- Entrepreneurs are *confident* and emotionally stable. They deal well with stress and adapt quickly. They feel comfortable with ambiguity, so that changing circumstances are viewed as opportunities to be seized, rather than threats to be feared. They recover quickly from failure and learn from their setbacks.
- Entrepreneurs have an **objective approach** to relationships. This means that they are more concerned with how another person performs rather than with their feelings.
- Entrepreneurs are often said to be **risk takers**. This does not mean that they take foolish risks, however. Their attitude towards risk may perhaps be captured by a famous aphorism of General George

S. Patton. "Take calculated risks," he said, but then added, "That is quite different from being rash."

MARKET RESEARCH: IS YOUR IDEA GOING TO WORK?

You think you have what it takes to be an entrepreneur, and you have an idea that you think shows great promise. Before you rush out and go into business, however, you need to think critically and systematically about the *viability* of your idea. You may think it is great, but how will consumers actually receive your product? How will competitors respond to it? Answering such questions is the province of **market research**, the art and science of collecting and making sense of information about your customers and market. Assessing the viability of your firm will also be useful when you get into business. It will provide a detailed list of things you need to do and alert you to potential problems. In

Bill Gates, founder of Microsoft, and the late Steve Jobs (left), the founder of the Apple Computer, exhibited many of the classic personality traits of the entrepreneur. *(Photo by Joi Ito. Wikipedia)*

The Entrepreneur Quiz

This is a quiz taken from a neat website, AllTheTests.com and can be accessed at (http://www.allthetests.com/quiz07/dasquiztd.php3?testid=1076428333). It is short and entertaining, but gets at many of the attributes that researchers have found to be correlated with entrepreneurial success. Just go through the following twenty questions, answering yes (Y) or no (N) to each.

1. Are you willing to undergo sacrifices to gain possible long-term rewards?   Y   N

2. Do you enjoy tackling a task without knowing all the potential problems?   Y   N

3. Are you prepared to make sacrifices in your family life and take a cut in pay to succeed in business?   Y   N

4. Are you willing to try a new way of doing things even if you are not fully sure you will succeed?   Y   N

5. Do you have a deep burning passion to make your idea work?   Y   N

6. Do you have a lot of energy and are you willing to work hard?   Y   N

7. Do you need less sleep when you are interested in a project?   Y   N

8. Do you keep your goal clearly in mind when there is something that you want?   Y   N

9. After a severe setback in a project, are you able to pick up the pieces and start over again?   Y   N

10. Can you accept failure without admitting defeat?   Y   N

11. Do you see opportunity in every difficulty?   Y   N

12. Are you ready to say yes when other people say no to you?   Y   N

13. Do you like the feeling of being in charge of other people?   Y   N

14. When you think of your future, do you ever envision yourself running your own business?   Y   N

15. Do you like to take responsibility and see things through?   Y   N

16. Do you believe that people must be masters of their own fate?   Y   N

17. Do you find yourself constantly thinking up new ideas?   Y   N

18. Do you enjoy finding an answer to a frustrating problem?   Y   N

19. Are you usually able to come up with more than one way to solve a problem?   Y   N

20. Do you come up with an innovative way of doing things?   Y   N

addition it may give you some ideas about **marketing strategy**, how to market your product in the best way to achieve your objectives. Having such a strategy in place will be important in convincing a bank, or any other potential source of capital, to lend you money to get started.

Assessing Market Feasibility, Part I: Fundamental Questions
In assessing the viability of your idea you have ask yourself some hard, concrete questions.

Question 1: What Are My Target Markets?
It is a mistake to try to be all things to all people. In fact, it is essential to define your **target markets**, in other words, precisely who it is you are trying to serve and exactly what it is you intend to provide. You have limited resources, so you can't afford to waste your marketing dollars on reaching people who won't be interested in your product. Most successful firms practice **market segmentation**. This is the practice of sorting customers into identifiable groups.

The first advantage of segmentation is that it allows you to adjust your marketing strategy both to your financial circumstances and to the needs of each group. Consider our by now familiar example of the bicycle company. Suppose that there are two potential types of people who might want to buy your bikes. One group consists of upwardly mobile young professionals who are environmentally conscious, and who might want to ride a bike to work. The other group consists of teenagers and college students who love to ride mountain bikes on forest trails. The way you approach each group might be entirely different, in which case you would follow a **differentiated marketing mix**. To attract the first group, for example, you might place ads on the local public radio station; to attract the second group you might distribute fliers at the upcoming Extreme Downhill Mountain Bike Olympics. Often, new firms find themselves so cash-strapped that they can't afford a differentiated strategy. In that case, they might focus on one segment, pursuing a **concentrated marketing mix**. Our firm might decide to focus on selling to the young professionals, for example, because they might have more money to spend.

The second advantage of segmentation is that, by defining your market narrowly enough, you may be able to reduce the number of competitors on your turf. If no one else is providing exactly the same good or service that you are providing, you have a degree of monopoly power. Pushing this idea to its logical extreme, you arrive at **niche marketing**, where the price, quality, the marketing methods, and even the good itself are carefully tailored to suit the needs of a narrowly defined group. Our bicycle company, for example, offers very expensive, hand-crafted bicycles to discriminating bicycle buffs. In contrast, Schwinn or Giant might offer less expensive, well-crafted but mass-produced bikes. This is described, oxymoronically, as a **mainstream niche**. Niche marketing has become very popular in online marketing. It is inexpensive to set up a Website targeted at a very small customer base, composed of people who are interested in a very narrow product line. Such customers may become quite loyal. This generates a small but steady flow of income, which permits the creation of another specialized website, and so on.

How can you determine your target market? The answer depends upon whether you plan to serve customers (a "business-to-consumer," or **B2C** firm) or other firms (a "business-to-business, or **B2B** firm).

For B2C firms marketing researchers try to identify related groups of consumers by breaking the population down in different ways:

- **Demographic** segmentation divides the population into classes according to characteristics such gender, race, education, marital status, age, income, and ethnicity.
- **Psychographic** segmentation divides people into groups based upon their psychological and sociological behavior. Examples include social class (upper, middle, or lower), activities (reading, sports, travel, music, fitness, shopping, etc.), and attitudes (e.g., being environmentally concerned).
- **Geographical** segmentation, as the name suggests, organizes people by where they live and work.
- **Behavioral** segmentation is based upon observations about how people respond to certain products. This has become more important with the growth of the Internet. You can ask people up front to fill out consumer surveys online so as to tailor the product or service to their individual needs. Similarly, it is now possible to categorize Internet users by the types of sites they visit, how long they visit, and what sorts of ads they respond to.

For B2B firms, market researchers segment other firms in slightly different ways:

- **Geographical** segmentation also works for firms, because specific industries tend to be clustered in certain areas. There is a high concentration of high-tech firms in Silicon Valley, in California, for example. Similarly, almost all of the production of carpets in the United States occurs in Dalton, Georgia. The town has more than 150 carpet plants, and is called the "Carpet Capital of the World."
- **Customer-based** B2B segmentation is based upon the behavioral characteristics of the firms. Reconsider the example of our bicycle company. Its primary market may be to individuals, but it may also

try to get a contract providing bikes to the city police department. The ways in which it markets it bikes (as well as the prices it can charge) to individual people and to the city government will be very different.

- **Product-use-based** B2B segmentation works by classifying the ways in which different firms might use your product. Suppose, for example, that you make software for inventory management. The type of software that Wal-Mart might need would be very different from what the local pharmacy down the street requires.

Question 2: What Needs Among the People in Your Target Markets Will Your Product Answer?

It is often hard for new entrepreneurs to answer this question objectively. You are enthusiastic about your idea and assume that everyone else will be too. But it is not you who will be buying your product, so you need to put yourself in the consumer's shoes. If you are a B2C firm, how will the customer benefit when he or she buys your product? What need does it satisfy? If you are B2B firm, how will the firm you are targeting benefit from working with you?

To get a grasp of why consumers buy things it may help to use a conceptual framework developed by marketing theorists. These theorists assert that people buy things because of the **utility** the things they buy confer. "Utility" means the ability of a good or service to answer a consumer's wants or needs. A good or service may confer utility in several ways:

- **Form utility** is the benefit provided by the consumption a final good or service. For example, a restaurant provides a meal, a car dealership provides a new car, and so forth.
- **Time utility** is the benefit conferred on a person by having a good or service provided at a convenient *time*. Walgreen's pharmacy, for example, may offer 24-hour service, or USPS may offer same-day delivery.
- **Place utility** satisfies the desire of a consumer to get a good or service at a convenient *place*. For example, it is convenient to find an ATM in the mall or to find a taxi stand immediately adjacent to the baggage pickup at the airport.
- **Ownership utility** derives from the smooth exchange of the *title* to a good. If you are buying a new iPod, for example, you derive utility from being able to acquire it with as little hassle as possible.

If you are a B2C company you need to think carefully about where *your* product would fit into this taxonomy. If it doesn't fit into at least one of these categories, it just may not be a good idea. If it does, then you should think about how best to *tailor* the product, or the way in which it is provided, to increase the utility that your consumers might derive from it.

If you are a B2B company, the reasoning is starkly simple. A firm will purchase your product or service for only one of two reasons—either because it hopes that good or service will raise its revenues, or because that good or service will reduce its costs. You need to determine whether or how you can achieve either or both.

Question 3: Are These Needs Insufficiently Satisfied by Existing Firms?
Answering this question requires careful study of what your potential competitors are doing. Can you do things better? Provide better quality? Faster service? A better location? These questions are inextricably bound up with the search for **competitive advantage** that we discussed in the context of Porter's five-factor method in Chapter 4. What distinguishes you from the competition?

Question 4: Is Your Target Population Large Enough and Affluent Enough to Sustain Your Business?
Economists teach that the demand for a good depends both upon "willingness to pay" and "ability to pay." People may love your product, but if there aren't enough of these people or if they are too poor to buy it, then it is all for naught. To answer this question you need to engage in careful research into the economic circumstances of your target population.

Assessing Market Feasibility, Part II: Acquiring the Information You Need
There is an array of methods to acquire the information needed to answer the questions posed in Part I of this section. The fundamental distinction is between **primary data** and **secondary data**.

Primary Data
You collect primary data yourself. This can be accomplished in a number of ways. If you have already been in business for a while you can just observe what your customers do. You can use the data from scanners if you are in the retail business, for example. Computers have made the business of observing consumers incredibly sophisticated. By keeping large databases of information about consumers it is possible to use fancy statistical techniques called **data mining** to deduce trends in consumer behavior that can be used to improve marketing and set prices more effectively. In fact, if *personal* data can be isolated (through the use of frequent-customer cards, for example), then it may be possible to keep tabs on an *individual's* buying habits and tailor a marketing plan to him or her personally. Some stores are now even using **video mining**. This consists of literally watching what the customer does in the store on video—where he or she goes first in the store, how he or she reacts to advertising stimuli. These are powerful tools that have stimulated a growing debate about privacy.

The big limitation of observation is that it doesn't tell you *why* consumers do what they do. To answer that question you have to ask them. One way of doing this is to take surveys. Surveys may be taken by telephone, door-to-door, or online. There is a fine art to constructing a good survey, though. The sample of people surveyed has to be both large enough and representative enough to give a reliable picture of the actual population.

Another way of asking people what they want and why they want it is by conducting interviews or **focus groups**. A focus group is a small number of people who are interviewed and observed by a "facilitator." Focus groups are popular because they are fairly inexpensive. However, they are often abused. It is not possible to get reliable statistics about the population from samples of handfuls of people. The real strength of focus groups is not really in providing answers but in giving you clues about what questions to ask in larger scale (and more expensive) statistical studies (using surveys, for example).

Another possibility is conducting simple experiments. You can, for example, devise two versions of a product, or two different methods of marketing, and see how small groups of consumers respond to them. An extreme (and more expensive) version of this approach would be to see how an actual **test market** responds to your product.

Secondary Data

Secondary data has already been collected by someone else. There are all sorts of information out there, most of it now readily accessible due to the Internet. For starters, there is a tremendous amount of data about specific industries, which is provided by the federal government. For many years the Bureau of Labor Statistics published data on industries organized according to Standard Industrial Classification (SIC) codes. In the last decade, this has been supplanted by the North American Industry Classification System (NAICS), which was developed in conjunction with Mexico and Canada to allow comparability of data across the three countries. For example the six-digit NAICS code for bicycles (well, technically it is "motorcycles, bicycles, and parts") is 336991, and the corresponding SIC code is 3751. Go to the Bureau of the Census Website at www.census.gov/econ/index.html, click on "Manufacturing," then scroll down to "Annual Survey of Manufactures." You will find all sorts of data on the industry, 336991, including things like employment, productivity per worker, various sorts of costs, inventories, and shipments. This kind of information is vital not only for developing a sense of trends in the industry, but also for collecting evidence about the viability of your firm for potential investors. Another great resource for a wide variety of industry data is at the University of Cincinnati Business & Economics Library (www.libraries.uc.edu/research/subject_resource/business/research_res/industry_data.html#industryI.) A few additional generic tips round out this section:

- Study the websites of your competitors. Look carefully at what they sell, how they sell it, where they sell it, how it is distributed, and how they are organized.
- Study the websites of large firms in your industry. The owner of our imaginary bicycle company, for example, might reconnoiter Schwinn's website. Schwinn also produces exercise bikes. Should you follow suit? In addition to asking the same questions that you do for smaller competitors you can also look at publicly available financial statistics about the large firm. Financial information about the big players may tell you something about the economic health of the whole industry.
- Follow industry trade journals and blogs assiduously. Our bicycle maker would be remiss in not reading the *Bicycle Retailer and Industry News* every week, or keeping tabs on *The Recumbent Blog*.
- Google it!

SUMMARY

This chapter posed two difficult questions that a promising, would-be entrepreneur must ask before taking the plunge: Do I have the abilities and interests required for the task? Is my idea viable? To provide a systematic way of approaching the first question we surveyed the psychological characteristics of successful entrepreneurs. To answer the second, we enumerated a set of concrete questions that need to be addressed to assess the viability of any new firm. We then discussed how to get the information to answer these questions, and how that information can help formulate a marketing strategy.

Let's suppose that you've answered both questions in the affirmative: Yes, I want to do this. Yes, my idea will fly. The next problem, operationally, is *how* to set up your firm. That is the subject of the next chapter.

Further Reading

AllTheTests.com. Entrepreneur Quiz. Retrieved July 2010 from http://www.allthetests. com/quiz07/dasquiztd.php3?testid=1076428333.

Baron, J., and J. Hollingshead. "Making Segmentation Work." *Marketing Management.* January/February (2002), 24–28.

Bovée, C., J. Thrall, and M. Mescon, M. *Excellence in Business.* 3rd ed. Upper Saddle River, N.J.: Pearson, 2007.

BusinessMart. Advantages and Disadvantages of a Start-up Business. Retrieved July 2010 from http://buying.businessmart.com/advantages-disadvantages-of-a-start-up-business.php.

Carland, J., F. Hoy, W. Boulton, and J. Carland, J. "Differentiating Entrepreneurs from Small Business Owners: A Conceptualization." *Academy of Management Review*, 9, no. 3 (1984): 354–359.

Glick-Smith, J. Successful Entrepreneurs. *Intercom* (July/August 1999).

Junior Achievement's 2009 Teens and Entrepreneurship Survey. Retrieved July 2010 from http://www.ja.org/files/polls/JA-Teen-Entrepreneurial-Poll-09.pdf.

Kinsley, M., and C. Clarke, C. *Creative Capitalism: A Conversation with Bill Gates, Warren Buffett, and Other Economic Leaders.* New York: Simon & Schuster, 2008.

Lowery, Y. *Minorities in Business: A Demographic Review of Minority Business Ownership*, Small Business Administration Office of Advocacy (2007). Retrieved June 2010 from http://www.sba.gov/advo/research/rs298tot.pdf.

———. *Women in Business: A Demographic Review of Women's Business Ownership*, Small Business Administration Office of Advocacy (2006). Retrieved June 2010 from http://www.sba.gov/advo/research/rs280tot.pdf.

Peterson, R. *Principles of Marketing.* Delhi Global Media. 2007.

Schumpeter, J. *Capitalism, Socialism, and Democracy.* New York: Harper, 1942 (reprinted 1975).

Small Business Administration. Are You Ready to Start a Business? (1942). Retrieved June 2010 from http://www.sba.gov/assessmenttool/index.html.

Wolfe, L. Be a Woman Entrepreneur—Start Your Own Business. About.com: Women in Business. Retrieved June 2010 from http://womeninbusiness.about.com/od/startingasmallbusiness/u/startups.htm.

CHAPTER 6

GOING INTO BUSINESS

Going into business for yourself, becoming an entrepreneur,
is the modern equivalent of pioneering on the old frontier.
—Paula Nelson, author

I like to tell people all of our products and businesses go
through three phases. There's vision, patience, and execution.
—Steve Ballmer, CEO of Microsoft

In Chapter 5 we tackled difficult questions about becoming an entrepreneur. Is this really what you want to do? Do you really have the aptitude for it? What exactly will be the product or service you provide and to whom will you provide it? Is your idea feasible? Let us suppose that, after much thought, you have arrived at satisfactory answers to these questions. You decide to take the plunge and start your own business. How do you go about doing it?

This chapter surveys the essential steps for getting up and running, and we'll consider them sequentially. First, having determined your target markets, you will need to decide how to *market* your product to those markets. Second, you will need to *estimate your costs* of production. Third, you will need to figure out how to acquire capital to *finance* the start-up and initial operations. Fourth, there are a number of *legal hoops* to jump through. Finally, you will need to develop a **business plan** that nails down much your preparatory work. This will not only help you step back to see the business strategically, but will also be indispensable in attracting investors.

MARKETING

To provide a framework for analyzing these steps, let's return to the aspiring owner of our bicycle company. He has done his homework and after careful analysis has determined that he can segment two target markets. One consists of young, professionals aged 25 to 45 (demographic segmentation), living downtown (geographical segmentation), with a "green" orientation (psychographic segmentation). The other consists of high school and college students (demographic segmentation), living mostly in the suburbs (geographical segmentation), with a strong interest in fitness and outdoor sports (psychographic segmentation). By studying industry publications and government statistics, our entrepreneur ascertains that the overall industry is flourishing, and that both target populations have sufficient income to buy his bikes. Before he sets up shop, though, he needs to devise a **marketing strategy**. Having this in hand will help him establish a competitive advantage and impress potential investors. How should he build a strategy? Marketing experts teach that the **marketing mix** of a firm has four components. Otherwise known as the **four P's of marketing**, this mix consists of product, price, place, and promotion.

Product

Product consists of the product itself, as well as other attributes such as quality and service. By determining his target markets, our bicycle maker has also narrowed the products he will provide: (1) high-quality ten-speeds to the urban professionals, who will use his bikes to commute to work; and (2) high-quality mountain bikes to the students, who will use them for weekend trips to the nearby national forest. In both cases he wants to capture the upper end of the market, so he will provide a lifetime warranty and free service.

Price

Price is a critical and difficult thing to establish. Set it too high and you may lose business, set it too low and you may lose revenue. Although your economics books will offer some deep insights into pricing, prices in practice are often set by one or more of the following methods, and by trial and error.

- **Demand pricing** is based upon extracting some of the value that consumers derive from using the product. One classic example is the practice of **price discrimination**, which means charging different prices of the same good to different people or in different markets, depending upon their willingness to pay.

- It is always wise to watch the pricing strategies of your competition. If there is little **product differentiation** across competitors, and you are entering a market where consumers have become accustomed to a certain price range, you may have little choice but to set a price comparable to that charged by competitors.
- **Cost-plus** pricing is a method that involves setting price at a fixed amount above costs per unit. This is simple, requires little information, and ensures that all costs are covered, leaving a **profit margin** over and above costs. However, this method is very mechanical and ignores information about consumers' demand for the good. It also precludes strategic responses to competitors' prices. A closely related method is **mark-up pricing**, which involves "marking up" the price above costs per unit, given knowledge of the demand for the good.

Our bicycle producer will succeed by making a product of such quality that he can differentiate it from those of his competitors. Furthermore the demand for his hand-crafted bikes may be fairly insensitive to price increases (what your economics books will call an "inelastic demand"). In fact a high price might even be taken as a signal of quality—owning such an expensive bike may be a status symbol. So the bike maker may start with a demand-pricing strategy, setting high prices in both markets, but not out of line with those of other specialty bike makers.

Place
Place, or **distribution**, is where the product is sold and how it is distributed to customers. Examples of distribution channels include sales to wholesalers, retailers, or directly to customers. The bike maker has no intention of competing with big firms like Schwinn or Giant, so he won't place his bikes in retail outlets like Wal-Mart or Costco. Instead, he will sell directly to his customers. He might build an art-deco show room downtown where the young professionals can study the merchandise while sipping on complimentary cappuccinos; he might build another showroom, adjacent to the university, where local garage bands will play each Saturday after a football game.

Promotion
Promotion is the art of spreading the word about the product. Promotion is multifaceted and may enter into every phase of the operation of the firm. It obviously encompasses **advertising** (on the Internet, newspapers, television, and so on). But it also involves details like packaging and the timing of public relations campaigns to coincide with new product development. Arguably, the quality of the product itself is part of promotion, because news of quality is spread by **word of mouth,** and people who value high quality, hand-crafted merchandise will talk with each other. The bike maker will eschew undifferentiated advertising,

so he won't send out flyers in the mail or place ads on television. He will create a sophisticated website. He will connect with the young professionals by advertising on public radio, in swanky magazines, and in the newsletter of the local bar association. He will connect with students by placing ads in the school paper, distributing flyers at football games, and hosting an annual battle of the bands.

ESTIMATING COSTS

By studying your potential market you have devised a marketing plan and have a rough idea of what your sales might be. Now you need to forecast how much it will *cost* you to satisfy this demand. How can you estimate your start-up costs? To answer this question we need to apply the concepts that were developed way back in Chapter 3.

The idea is very simple: You want to add up all of the costs of going into business and the costs of operating your firm for an initial period. Putting this idea into practice, however, is rather complicated. There are many different costs to keep track of, and there are numerous conceptual and accounting fine points to remember. The good news is that the job of keeping track of all these things has been tremendously simplified because many templates and spreadsheets for this purpose are now available online. Do a Google search for "start-up costs," and you will be amazed at what you can find. There is some variation in these programs, but we will build our discussion here around one that is particularly clear and simple to use—a program provided by the Missouri Business Development Program, which can be accessed at http://www.missouribusiness.net/ sbtdc/docs/startup_annual_expense.pdf.

The first thing to remember is that you need to maintain a strict distinction between start-up costs proper and the continuing costs of operation after you are in business. **Start-up costs** consist *only* of once-and-for-all expenses that occur before the first month you are in business. **Ongoing monthly costs** consist of expenses beginning with the first month of operation. What really matters to you, of course, is the sum of these two things. However, accounting rules require that you keep them in separate budgets because ongoing expenses need to appear in the first year's profit and loss statement. Be careful not to count costs twice; list a given expense either in "start-up" or in "ongoing," but not in both.

Table 6.1 presents categories of costs, both start-up and ongoing, listed by the Missouri Business Development Program. Your job as a new entrepreneur will be to assign dollar values to each category. Some of them are self-explanatory; others are not, but we will discuss some of the fine points of these costs below.

- It is important to distinguish between **start-up expenditures** and **start-up assets**. Expenditures are monies spent to acquire *current* goods or services; an asset yields *future* benefits. For example the category **Cash (Working Capital)** is an asset because it consists of

TABLE 6.1
One-time Set-up Costs and Ongoing Monthly Expenses

One-time set-up costs	Ongoing Monthly Expenses
Legal, Accounting, & Professional Services	Salaries & Wages
Advertising & Promotions	Outside Services
Deposits for Utilities	Office Supplies & Postage
Licenses & Permits	Dues & Subscriptions
Prepaid Insurance	Donations
Salary & Wages	Rent
Payroll Taxes	Telephone
Truck & Vehicle	Utilities
Travel	Loan Payments
Tools & Supplies	Interest
Furniture & Fixtures	Depreciation
Machines & Equipment	Advertising & Promotions
Building Improvements	Truck & Vehicle
Land & Buildings	Travel
Starting Inventory	Payroll Taxes
Cash (Working Capital)	Taxes, Licenses & Permits
Other	Legal & Accounting Services

money you set aside in your (the firm's) bank account to sustain operations in the future. Similarly, **inventories** are assets because they consist of goods that you set aside in expectation of selling them in the future. The cost of selling the inventoried goods in the future can be counted as expenses. The distinction is vital for tax purposes because *expenditures are deductible against income, while assets are not.* For this reason it is often desirable to "expense" costs of research and development rather than "capitalizing" them.

- Calculating salaries and wages of your employees is fairly straightforward. Recall the example of the costs of our bicycle company in Chapter 3. The firm expected to hire 5 workers, each of whom would work 160 hours per month for a wage of $15 per hours. The monthly wage bill was then $12,000 or $15 × 160 × 55.
- Calculating your own salary is trickier. There are two schools of thought about this. One might be called the "I'll pay myself what I am worth" school. This approach is based on the premise that you should pay yourself the **implicit costs** of going into business. By this reckoning you should compensate yourself by the amount that you would have made in an alternative career if you had not opened the business. In Chapter 3, for example, our bicycle maker gave up the legal profession to pursue a long-held dream. As an attorney, the owner of our bicycle company made $50,000 a month. Now, he might derive some non-pecuniary pleasure from owning his own business, so the actual implicit cost might only be $40,000. In this case, "I'll pay myself what I am worth" school would say he should pay himself $40,000 a month. The contending "I'll pay myself what I can" school would recommend a much smaller figure. It would admit that the owner should cover his implicit costs in the long haul, but that this might not be realistic initially. Most new firms take losses for months, if not years, before they ever turn a profit. Realistically, then, you should calculate your own personal budget to determine how much you *need* to pay your bills and feed the family. Accept this amount as your own salary at the start. When things get better, you can raise your pay as the profits of the firm grow.
- **Payroll taxes** (mostly for Social Security) normally amount to about 10 to 15 percent of the total payroll.
- **Depreciation** is the decline in the value of a piece of machinery as it ages. In practice this is usually calculated using tables constructed for each type of machinery. Remember that depreciation is tax deductible.
- **Interest** is your monthly payment on money you have borrowed.

You may recall from Chapter 3 that costs may be categorized as fixed or variable. **Fixed costs** are the same regardless of how much you produce whereas **variable costs** increase with the amount that you produce. Examples of fixed costs from our list of Start-up and Ongoing Monthly Expenses include travel, repairs and maintenance, rent, advertising and promotion, utilities, office supplies and postage, insurance, loan payments, and interest. Our bicycle firm in Chapter 3 had only one fixed cost, rent of $1,000 a month. Variable costs include wages and salaries, inventories, and truck and vehicle expenses. The only variable costs of the bicycle company were labor expenses. It cost $12,000 to produce 15 ten-speeds and 5 mountain bikes. To increase production, the firm would incur higher labor costs.

One last observation is in order. Try hard to minimize your set-up costs. Every dollar you save will increase your profits. Buy used office furniture and computers. Buy office supplies in bulk. Keep your wage costs down by offering your employees compensating perquisites, like flexible hours or serving them hand-made lattes at breaks. Be creative.

BREAK-EVEN ANALYSIS

Given the high failure rate of start-ups, a crucial question for you (and your investors) is "Will I make it?" What can help decide this matter is a clear, objective measure of "making it." **Break-even analysis** provides just that, because it allows you predict *how much you need to sell* in order to turn a profit, or break even. This analysis is built upon a simple application of concepts developed in Chapter 3 and in the previous section on costs.

To begin, you must recall two things. First, profit is the difference between revenue and cost. Second, cost can be divided into fixed and variable components. It follows that we can express profit as *Profit = Revenue – Variable Cost – Fixed Cost*.

Now you'll have to suffer through a little algebra. Let's suppose for simplicity that the firm sells only one good. In this case, its **revenue** is the amount that it sells multiplied by the price per unit, *Revenue = Price × Quantity*. Similarly, variable cost is the **variable cost per unit** (what economists call "average variable cost") multiplied by the quantity, or *Variable Cost = Variable Cost per Unit × Quantity*.

Using these facts we can rewrite profit as *Profit = Price × Quantity – Average Variable Cost per Unit × Quantity – Fixed Cost*. Now ask yourself the following question: What quantity do I have to sell just to make zero profit? This quantity is called the **break-even quantity**. You can find it by setting *Profit* equal to zero in the preceding equation and solving for *Quantity*. The answer is given by the break even formula:

$$\text{Break-Even Quantity} = \frac{\text{Fixed Cost}}{\text{Price} - \text{Variable Cost per unit}}$$

The denominator is called the "contribution" of production to profit, or *Contribution = Price – Variable Cost per Unit*, so the break even formula is sometimes expressed as

$$\text{Break-Even Quantity} = \frac{\text{Fixed Cost}}{\text{Contribution}}$$

The higher your overhead costs, the more you need to sell to break even. Set aside the algebra and think about what this means. Basically it means that if you can achieve the break-even quantity you will be making just enough money to start making a profit. To put it another way, every unit that you sell in excess of the break even quantity is money in your pocket. In fact the difference between the amount that you actually sell and the break even quantity is the called the **margin of safety**:

Margin of Safety = Actual Quantity Sold – Break-Even Quantity

The break-even quantity is of great importance for two reasons. First, once you are in business, you will need to keep a constant eye on the margin of safety. If it turns negative you will either have to find a way to reduce costs or borrow more to cover the loss. Second, the break-even quantity is of vital interest to potential investors, because it gives them an idea of the minimum scale of operations you need to achieve to stay in business. This leads us to our next topic, acquiring investment capital.

FINANCING THE START-UP

Start-up **financial capital** is the money you need to get from lenders or investors to set up your company. In order to acquire this financing you must confront two crucial questions: (1) How much capital do I need? and (2) How can I get it?

How Much Do I Need?

To determine your financing needs you must construct a **start-up budget**. Here too, it is easy to find spreadsheets online. The typical start-up budget looks something like the one presented in the sidebar.

The total costs of starting your company consist of two parts. First there are the **One-time Set-up Costs** outlined in the previous section. Second, there

Start-up Budget

+ One-time Set-up Costs

+ Continuing Costs

– Income

– Cash Available from Savings

= End Balance

are the ongoing costs of operation once you are set up. To calculate these, take the *monthly* **ongoing costs** from the previous section and multiply these by the number of months you expect it will to take you to get established, let's say a year (12 months).

Your **income** consists of all the money that you plan to bring in over the course of your first year in business. This income also comes in two parts. One is your **business income**, which is the annual revenue (or sales). The other is **household income**, money you earn from other sources, like a second job. To estimate your business income over the first year, ask yourself how much you expect to sell each month of each type of good or service, add this up, and multiply by twelve. For example, each month our bicycle store in Chapter 3 expected to sell 15 ten-speeds per month for $2,500 apiece and 5 mountain bikes for $5,000 apiece. Its expected monthly revenue was thus $62,500 or ($2,500 × 15) + ($5,000 × 5). So the company's anticipated income from the first year is then $750,000 (not bad!). A cautionary note here is that you should always be conservative in your projections. It is safer to underestimate your sales than to overestimate them.

The difference between your costs and your income is essentially (except for household income) the negative of your profit. In other words, it is a measure of the *loss* you might expect to face in the first year. You can cover some of this loss by drawing down your own savings, which is the budget category listed in the sidebar as **Cash Available from Savings**. If you can't cover the losses by yourself, then you are left with a **Year End Balance** that has to be financed somehow. The Year End Balance is the minimum amount of capital that you have to acquire.

How Do I Get It?

There are a variety of sources for financing. We will discuss each in turn and briefly describe their advantages and disadvantages.

Self-finance

The simplest option is to **self-finance**, which means drawing upon your own assets or wealth. The advantage of self-financing is that it is usually fairly easy to accomplish. The disadvantage is that you put your personal financial security at risk. Successful entrepreneurs can take a fairly ruthless view of this trade-off: They see putting your life savings on the table as a rite of passage, one that shows how badly you want to succeed.

So how do you go about self-financing? There are a variety of ways. You can sell an asset (like a car or a boat) or borrow from your family or friends. Alternatively, you can take out a home-equity loan or borrow against your life insurance. (Note that this applies only to whole life insurance, which has an investment component that accumulates a cash value, against which you may borrow. Term life insurance only pays off at the death of the insured and has no investment component.)

If you have already been employed, another option might be to withdraw money from your 401(k) plan. A 401(k) is a kind of tax-deferred savings account that employers can set up for their employees. Normally there are severe penalties for withdrawing money your 401(k) before retirement, but federal law permits withdrawals from 401(k)s to finance new businesses. Be aware, however, that these withdrawals are taxed heavily. Furthermore, this is a complicated option; doing it properly usually requires the expensive services of lawyers and accountants.

Another common form of self-financing is just to put everything on your credit cards. Fully half of start-ups rely upon credit cards for financing, and it is easy to see why. Credit cards are flexible, easy to use, and very quick. The downside here is that they can also be very dangerous. If your business does poorly, you can get trapped in mounting interest payments on your credit card debt.

Bank Financing

Another possibility is to take out a bank loan. These loans may be "intermediate term" (up to three years in duration) or "long term" (more than three, up to twenty years). In either case you are obligated to pay interest (usually a fixed rate) until maturity.

There are, however, several problems with bank financing. To begin with, banks rarely finance start-ups. When they do, they require collateral, usually equipment or capital. Moreover, getting a bank loan is a slow process and takes a lot of paperwork. Finally, banks won't cover the full amount needed. They usually require 25 to 30 percent of the start-up costs to be covered by the borrower from personal sources.

Venture Capitalists

Venture capitalists (VCs) are companies that specialize in pooling funds from institutional investors (insurance companies or pension funds, for example) and from rich individual investors to finance promising start-ups. VCs typically invest large amounts of money, anywhere from $500,000 to $10 million. The caveat here is that it is hard to get VC support, because VC investors are very selective. They are usually interested only in firms that show great potential for growth, where "great" means achieving millions of dollars of sales within the first five years or so. As a result, although VCs have been quite active in specific, high-growth sectors (such as high-tech, information technology, biomedical, and digital media), they finance only a small percentage of start-ups. Their support also comes at a cost: They make their money by selling their stake in the company once it takes off. This means that they require a large share of the

Something to Consider When Banks Won't Lend

The difficulty of getting bank loans for start-ups prompted the Small Business Administration (SBA) to starts its **microlending** program in 1992. As the name suggests, microloans are small loans, ranging from a few hundred to a few thousand dollars. These funds generally pay for equipment, furniture, and other start-up expenses. The program is usually offered in coordination with non-profit organizations, most of which have a local focus. For example, Accion Texas provides start-up loans in the state of Texas. Other organizations connected to the microlending program have national, or even international, missions. For example, the Association for Enterprise Opportunity encourages microlending in the United States and Mexico. Although it is not hard to get approval for a microloan, it may be hard to find a microlender, and the amounts provided are usually fairly small.

equity of the firm (sometimes up to 60 percent); the newer the firm, the greater the equity stake they will require. VCs also have a direct interest in the management of the firm, so they provide management advice. In essence VCs are viable only for firms with enormous growth potential and for entrepreneurs who are willing to surrender a great deal of control to the VC.

Angel Investors

Angel investors are wealthy individuals who provide start-up financing. Like VCs, they make their money by investing in a fledgling firm and selling their share once the firm has become successful. Like VCs, they look for firms with high growth potential, from 30 to 40 percent a year. They typically invest less than VCs, but they are likely to stay with the firm longer. Like VCs they often get directly involved in the management of the firm; sometimes they charge management consulting fees over and above the equity investment. Angel investors are useful for start-up firms that expect to grow quickly and are seeking moderate infusions of capital. As with VCs, the downside of angels is that they demand a lot of control in the operations of the firms they invest in.

Most angel investors have a local focus, so you can find connections to them through your local Chamber of Commerce. Local bankers, lawyers, and accountants may also have the right connections. Angels have also gotten together to form **angel networks** or **angel clubs** to exchange news about, and coordinate investments in, new firms. A good source on angels is *Inc.* magazine's Directory of Angel Investors, which can be accessed at www.inc.com.

Going Public
Another potential source of financing is to **go public**, which means selling stock on the open market. The initial sale of stock by a firm is called an **Initial Public Offering (IPO)**. Going public is a big step. On the one hand, it allows access to vast amounts of capital if people buy the stock. On the other hand, it might yield nothing if people don't buy it—a very real possibility for start-ups about which the public knows little. Furthermore, the actual mechanics of an IPO are time-consuming and expensive. In general, going public is usually not the best financing option for small start-ups unless they offer something high profile enough to attract a lot of attention and public exposure.

The Small Business Administration
The Small Business Administration (SBA) does not finance start-ups directly but is included here because it does something very closely related by providing the fledgling entrepreneur with a loan guarantee. What this means in practice is that you apply for a loan at the bank. The SBA then guarantees from 50 to 80 percent of the loan, up to a maximum of $2 million. The primary SBA loan program is called the 7(a) program, although there is also a 7(m) that offers microloans through community-based, non-profit lenders. This is an important source of money for start-ups. To give you some sense of just how important, consider that SBA grants helped start FedEx, Intel, and Apple Computer. To see more about what the SBA offers, check out its Website, at www.sba.gov/financialassistance/borrowers/guaranteed/.

LEGAL HURDLES
As you might expect, going into business involves jumping through a number of legal hoops. There are hoops at the federal, state, and local levels, but you must be careful not to miss any of them.

Federal Hoops
The Federal government by and large does not require too much of a start-up. However, there two things you need to do:

- Make sure you apply for an **Employer Identification Number (EIN)**, sometimes called a **Federal Tax Identification Number**. The EIN is the number with which the Internal Revenue Service (IRS) will recognize your firm.
- In most cases the Federal government does not require licenses or permits. However, if you are in any of the following businesses you should look into how it is regulated or licensed at the federal level: investment advising, drug manufacturing, meat production, broadcasting, ground transportation, or sales of alcohol, tobacco, or

firearms. Check with the Federal Trade Commission (FTC) to see if you need a license.

State Hoops
At the state level things begin to get more complicated.

- If your state has an income tax (and most do), you will need a state EIN.
- If your state has a sales tax, you must acquire a sales tax permit.
- If you plan to hire workers (as we have seen, the vast majority of start-ups do not), you will also have to register with the state as an employer. This is important because you will be contributing to unemployment insurance for your employees.
- In addition there are all sorts of business licenses. Some are required of certain occupations or professions (contractors, doctors, barbers, debt collectors, etc.). The list varies from state to state, so you will have to see if you are on it. Some licenses are required for the sale of certain products in almost all states (liquor, lottery tickets, gasoline, firearms).

Local Hoops
At the local level the regulations and licenses seem to proliferate.

- Most cities require a license to do business within the city limits. The location of your business has to satisfy local zoning restrictions, unless you apply for a **variance** from the planning commission. A variance is an exception to zoning laws, granted by the city to a firm.
- Depending upon your business you may need permits from the fire department, or from the relevant air pollution or water pollution control authorities.
- If you plan to post billboards or signs, you will also have to apply for a sign permit and abide by regulations on the size and location of signage.

There is another start-up decision that seems very simple but has legal complications that may reach across all three levels of government: What will you name your company? If you decide to be a sole proprietor, most states require that you use your own name as the name of your business. You must also decide whether your "trade name" (the one you use in advertising) will be exactly the same as the full legal name. You must be very, very careful that your name, or something close it, isn't used by someone else. Just recall the epic contest

(continues on page 98)

Typical Business Plan

COVER SHEET

State clearly who you are and how you may be contacted (address, phones, e-mail). Identify exactly who wrote the plan and give the date it was written.

EXECUTIVE SUMMARY OR STATEMENT OF PURPOSE

This is where you sell your idea. It short and sweet, no more than one page in length, preferably less. Explain *succinctly* what your firm will do and why you think it will be profitable. Remember that your investors are there to turn a profit, so go straight to the bottom line. Tell them how and why they will make money by investing in your firm.

THE BUSINESS

Now go into greater detail about what you will do. Many of the concepts we have encountered in previous chapters will come into play.

Explain clearly what you intend to do. Define exactly what your product or service will be and the **target market** it will serve. Don't just say that *you* think this a great idea; explain precisely how it will satisfy specific needs of your customers. Specify when (hours of operation) and where you will operate.

Describe the structure of your company. Say explicitly that it is a start-up. Explain the business form (sole proprietorship, partnership, corporation, from Chapter 2) you have chosen and why.

Describe the market that you will be entering. This is where you can apply the insights you gained from Porter's five-factor analysis (Chapter 4). Discuss the presence or absence of barriers to entry, the strength of buyer and supplier power, the threat of substitutes, and the degree of competitive rivalry in the market. Include what you've learned by studying the behavior of your potential competitors.

Describe your **marketing strategy** (discussed at the beginning of this chapter). How will you reach and serve your target market? Discuss the **four P's** in detail. Give a clear definition of your **product**, explain how you will **price** it, how you will **place** (or distribute) it, and how you will **promote** it.

Describe your operating procedures and personnel. Provide personal histories of the owners and managers, with special emphasis on relevant professional experience. Explain how many employees you will need and what they will be doing. Describe the organizational structure of the firm—who makes what decisions, how performance is measured and monitored, and how performance is rewarded.

FINANCIAL ISSUES

In this part of the plan you will summarize your projected costs, revenues, profits, and financial needs.

Note any outstanding loan applications or describe the loans for which you are applying.

Provide a list of the capital equipment and supplies you will need for your initial operations. Much of this information will come from your estimates of set-up and continuing costs (also described earlier in this chapter).

Provide a projected **balance sheet**. A balance sheet constitutes a picture of the financial condition of the firm at a moment in time. It consists of three parts: assets, liabilities and net worth or equity.

- **Assets** are broken down into "current assets" and "long-term" assets. "Current" assets consist of (1) cash, (2) the value of current inventories, and (3) accounts receivable, which is money that is expected to be received from credit accounts given to customers. "Long-term" assets are less liquid. They consist essentially of (1) capital and equipment, and (2) illiquid financial investments (which start-ups rarely have).

- **Liabilities** are debts that you owe. They also can be "current" or "long-term." "Current" liabilities consist of (1) accounts payable, which is money you need to pay on credit accounts, (2) accrued liabilities, which is money you owe but haven't paid yet on overhead and salaries, and (3) taxes. "Long term" liabilities consist of payments on bonds, mortgages, and notes.

- **Net worth** or **equity** (if you issue stock) is the difference between assets and liabilities.

Using your cost estimates, undertake a **break-even analysis** (also covered in this chapter). This will give a potential investor an idea of the minimum scale of operations you will need to achieve in order to turn a profit.

Provide a **pro forma income statement**. An income statement is a measure of profit or loss over a given period, whereas "pro forma" is just a fancy way of saying "projected." To project your profits or losses, use the information on revenues and continuing expenses from the start-up budget. However, you should develop forecasts for both revenues and costs for a couple of years into the future. Be very clear about the assumptions you make in developing these forecasts. For example, if you assume that sales will grow by 3 percent a year, but that costs will increase by 2 percent per year, you need to make your assumptions explicit, and justify them.

SUPPORTING DOCUMENTATION

Provide copies of lease agreements, letters of intent from suppliers, or licenses.

(continued from page 95)

between "Apple Records" of Beatles fame and "Apple Computers" of Steve Jobs fame over the use of the word "apple." Many trade names are not recorded nationally, so you should execute a broader search to make sure you aren't stepping on anyone's toes. Trade names can be registered with the Department of State of your state or with the United States Patent Office.

THE BUSINESS PLAN

You have done a lot of homework on a variety of aspects of setting up your firm. You've studied your market and determined the viability of your firm. You've settled on a marketing strategy, estimated your costs and revenues, determined your break-even point, and reconnoitered the legal terrain. Now there is one last hurdle that will integrate everything you've gleaned from your research. You have to write a **business plan**, a written summary of what your firm will do and how, along with estimates of its costs, revenue, and profitability. This serves two purposes. On the one hand, you will use it to attract potential investors. On the other hand, by forcing you to review and integrate your preparatory research, it will help you to refine and direct the way you will run your business.

Normally, a business plan is approximately 20 to 30 pages long. In keeping with its dual purposes, it often appears in several different forms. The business plan *per se* is distributed to banks or investors. However, many firms keep a much longer and more detailed version as a "work in progress," to which the owners can return for inspiration and guidance. Many firms now also keep a version online, which can be accessed by anyone interested in the firm. Some firms also keep a mini-plan, no more than 10 pages in length, which can be distributed to customers. Experts suggest that you should spend at least six months writing the plan.

Like the set-up budget, there is no single, prescribed way of organizing a business plan. However, the one recommended by the SBA is as good as any, so we are using its template (go to www.sba.gov/smallbusinessplanner/plan/write-abusinessplan/SERV_WRRITINGBUSPLAN.html) to guide our discussion. We will deviate from it in places and provide some commentary. The sidebar for this section illustrates what a typical business plan should look like.

SUMMARY AND SOME ADVICE

Going into business requires a lot of work and strategic planning. You have to develop a marketing strategy, anticipate your sales and costs, realistically assess your profitability, and attract potential investors. The business plan is your opportunity to step back and put all of these pieces of the puzzle together. With the plan in hand you are ready to go.

To conclude this chapter we present some specific advice, which was offered to *young* entrepreneurs by Elizabeth Kountze in *Kiplinger* (www.kiplinger.com/columns/starting/archive/2006/st0504.htm). In a column titled "Six Steps to Starting Your Own Business," Kountze expounds on some basic principles of getting started. She cites an amazingly successful young entrepreneur named Max Durovic as an example of these principles at work. Max went into business at age 18, while a sophomore at Georgetown University. He established Aarow Advertising, a company that uses teens and college students to carry sandwich-board ads on the street for local retailers. The students spin and throw the signs to attract attention. In 2010 Max had 350 employees in 10 cities, with sales of about $4.5 million. Here are the lessons Ms. Kountze says we can learn this young entrepreneur.

- *Get some experience.* It is always a good idea to spend some time in the business you are entering. You may not like working for someone else, but Ms. Kountze says you should think of it as "a paid research position." She broadens the notion of experience to include classes in business, management, or entrepreneurship. Max was a major in International Business and Marketing and says that his actual business experience "brought the classes to life."
- *Build a Winning Team.* Look for people who complement your skills and share your passion. Max, for example, teamed up with a fellow student from Georgetown and one of her friends.
- *Fight Inexperience with Advice.* Don't be afraid to ask for help and mentoring. Max asked one of his professors at Georgetown for advice, and still employs him as a consultant. You can also get help online. For example, the small business counseling organization SCORE (http://www.score.org/index.html) promotes a network of over 10,000 (mostly retired) mentors for would-be entrepreneurs. Entrepreneurs can support and advise each other at the website www.YoungEntrepreneur.com.
- *Write a Bulletproof Business Plan.* At the risk of sounding repetitious, this is vital for two reasons: First, it really forces you to think through your plans. Second, it is crucial to raising capital. "One of the biggest mistakes a young entrepreneur can make," says Ms. Kountze, "is simply failing to write a business plan."
- *Raise Money.* Here Ms. Kountze offers very concrete advice. First, overestimate your costs. Second, try to minimize the amount of personal money you risk. Third, "steer clear of credit cards." Fourth, try to get a loan at a bank first—if you have a good credit rating and request a loan of less than $50,000, you will probably get it; if not, you can still profit from the banker's advice.

- *Follow the money.* This means starting the business with enough of a cash cushion to sustain your early losses. It also means scrupulously keeping track of your revenues and costs.
- Last but not least, Ms. Kountze emphasizes that you should stay focused on two over-arching goals in the first year. First, meet or exceed your expectations. Second, treat your customers right.

Further Reading

Allon, J., and the editors of *Victoria Magazine. Turn Your Passion Into Profits: How to Start the Business of Your Dreams.* New York: Hearst Books, 2001.

Bovée, C., J. Thrall, and M, Mescon. *Excellence in Business.* 3rd ed. Upper Saddle River, N.J.: Pearson, 2007.

Brickley, J., J. Zimmerman, and C. Smith. C. *Managerial Economics & Organizational Architecture.* 5th ed. New York: McGraw-Hill/Irwin, 2008.

BusinessMart, Advantages and Disadvantages of a Start-up Business. Retrieved July 2010 from http://buying.businessmart.com/advantages-disadvantages-of-a-start-up-business.php.

Entrepreneur Centre. "Entrepreneur Training Guide: Catching the Wave." Retrieved July 2010 from http://www.loginstitute.ca/entrepreneur/index.php?id=24&level=4

Meiners, R., A. Ringleb, and F. Edwards, F. *The Legal Environment of Business.* Mason, Ohio: Southwestern Publishing Company, 2000.

Missouri Business Development Program. Start-up and Annual Expenses Worksheets. Retrieved July 2010 from http://www.missouribusiness.net/sbtdc/docs/startup_annual_expense.pdf.

Narayanan, M., and V. Nanda., V. *Finance for Strategic Decision Making: What Non-financial Managers Need to Know.* New York: John Wiley & Sons, 2008.

Peterson, R. *Principles of Marketing.* Delhi Global Media, 2007.

Small Business Administration. Are You Ready to Start a Business? Retrieved June 2010 from http://www.sba.gov/assessmenttool/index.html.

Small Business Administration. Guaranteed Loan Programs. Retrieved June 2010 from http://www.sba.gov/financialassistance/borrowers/guaranteed/.

Small Business Administration. Small Business Planner, Retrieved June 2010 from http://www.sba.gov/smallbusinessplanner/index.html.

Small Business Administration Office of Advocacy. (2009). Frequently Asked Questions. Retrieved June 2010 from http://web.sba.gov/faqs/faqindex.cfm?areaID=24.

CHAPTER 7

EXPANDING YOUR BUSINESS

He who moves not forward, goes backward.
—Johann Wolfgang von Goethe

If I'd had some set idea of a finish line,
don't you think I would have crossed it years ago?
—Bill Gates

Your business is now up and running. You are doing well and have been running at a profit for a couple of years. Sooner or later you will ask yourself whether the time has come to make your business bigger. The decision to expand is not one to be taken lightly. It is every bit as momentous as the decision to go into business in the first place and must be approached with the same forethought and planning. In this chapter we address some basic questions about "growing" your firm. Under what circumstances is it a good idea to expand? When is the best time to do so? How should you go about doing it?

SHOULD YOU EXPAND?
The decision to set up your company required a careful assessment of the costs and benefits of doing so. Now you need to revisit the same issues, because making your firm bigger may change it so much that in some ways it will become a "new" firm. Expansion has obvious economic and financial benefits and costs. In fact,

a good rule of thumb is that *you shouldn't even consider expansion unless you are currently making a profit.* Your current profitability may signal the possibility of future profitability; if you are operating at a loss, the reverse is likely to be true. Furthermore, just like start-ups, expanding firms often initially take losses, so you will need a financial cushion. Money, however, isn't everything. Expansion also entails what economists call "psychic" benefits and costs, psychological attributes that are unquantifiable but none the less real. Let us consider both factors.

Economic Aspects of the Decision to Expand

The essential criterion is that you should *consider expansion only if it promises to increase your profits.* Now recall the definition of profit from Chapter 3:

$$Profit = Revenue - Cost$$

Expanding the operations of the firm will necessarily increase costs. Looking at this formula, it should be apparent that expansion will only increase profit if it raises revenue by more than it raises costs. There are basically three ways this can happen.

1. You might be expecting demand for the products or services that you currently provide to increase. If this occurs, you might be able to sell more, or sell it at higher prices, or both, so that your revenues increase substantially. This might happen for any number of reasons, some of which are beyond your control. Perhaps the economy is coming out a recession, so consumers are starting to buy more. Or perhaps something has happened to change the way consumers look at your product. Suppose, for example, the government announces a new study establishing that bicycling is the single best form of aerobic exercise. Our bicycle manufacturer might anticipate a spike in demand. Sometimes, however, demand may increase as a result of strategic decisions by the firm itself. Maybe our bicycle company has worked so hard to produce the best bikes around that it has gained a reputation for quality. Brand loyalty for the company is strong and growing, so revenues are expected to grow.

   All of these are examples of where the demand in the same target market for the good has increased. It is also possible to expand by selling the same good to similar customers in different places, by expanding geographically. Max Durovic, the brilliant young entrepreneur you read about at the end of Chapter 6, is a great example. Starting from Georgetown, he expanded to universities across the country, knowing that the same demand and cost conditions were likely to pertain to most university communities.

2. You might try to branch out to sell a different type of product. This can also occur in a variety of ways. Sometimes firms try to sell new goods that require similar production techniques as their existing product line. The bicycle company might decide to sell stationary exercise bicycles, as well as conventional bicycles, for example. In other cases, firms engage in vertical mergers, not only to reduce their own costs but also to sell the intermediate good themselves. In Chapter 2, for example, we entertained the possibility that the bicycle firm might merge with the downstream sprocket producer. This might reduce the cost of the sprockets and also improve the reliability of the delivery. It would also allow the bicycle firm to sell sprockets itself, providing a new source of revenue.

Another way of branching out is to *look for clever ways of selling the same thing in different ways*. A classic example of this principle is baking soda. It is used for baking, toothpaste, household cleaning, and deodorizing; most recently, it is now being touted on certain blogs as a cure for cancer. One product selling in a multitude of forms.

3. You may be interested in adjusting or adapting to **economies of scale**. This, as you may recall from Chapter 2, is a situation in which increasing production will decrease costs per unit. Economies of scale may occur for a number of reasons:
   - It may be possible to spread the overhead costs of advertising over a larger amount of production.
   - The larger scale may reduce the cost of acquiring inputs, either by permitting purchases in bulk or by enhancing the firm's bargaining power with suppliers.
   - Managers may become more skilled if they are allowed to specialize in particular functional areas (marketing, accounting, finance, and so forth).

Be on the lookout for economies of scale, but do not jump to the conclusion that they always exist. They are common in some sectors (in particular in heavy industries, like the automobile industry), but less common in others (restaurants, for example). Furthermore, at some sufficiently large scale of operation, economies of scale may be more than offset by **diseconomies of scale**. These occur because the company gets so large that it has to spend more and more resources on administrative personnel, and workers spend more and more time sitting in meetings.

If you are thinking of producing new goods, there may also be **economies of scope** (also explained in Chapter 2). Economies of scope arise if it is cheaper to produce two goods together than it would be to produce them separately. By making exercise bikes as well as conventional bikes, for example, the bike company might be able to acquire belts, wheels, and oil at cheaper prices by purchasing them in bulk. A real-world example is the curious fact that hematology and cancer clinics are often housed in the same offices. This is because hematologists (who specialize in blood problems) often do advanced study in oncology (the study and treatment of cancer). It is cheaper to let the same doctors treat both types of disease than to have two separate clinics.

Bear in mind as well that there may be advantages in being small and *not* venturing out into new markets. On the one hand, if you nurture your niche market you may develop a loyal customer base and be able to charge higher prices. On the other hand, if you expand into bigger markets you may have to compete with larger firms and lose your customer base.

Non-economic Aspects of Expanding

Expansion will inevitably transform your firm into something very different from the firm you first created. It will change the way you run your business and may even change its objectives. In *Turn Your Passion Into Profits: How to Start the Business of Your Dreams*, Janet Allon and her co-authors posit that there are two questions you need to think about before expanding. Both get at the very reason you went into business in the first place, so it will take some soul-searching to answer them.

Question 1: Are you willing to play a less hands-on role in the expanded operation?

Expansion will reduce your ability to control operations in two ways. First, you will almost surely need to hire more employees. The vast majority of firms (some 21.7 million according to the Department of the Census) have no employees at all, so hiring even one or two is a big step. If you are opening a new store or a new plant, you will have to hire managers you can trust. You will have to be a personnel manager in addition to executing all of your other responsibilities. You will have to get used to meetings and administrative headaches. At a deeper level, you will have to learn to delegate, and let others share your responsibilities.

The second reason you may lose control is that your investors may demand it. Expanding your business is likely to attract or accelerate a higher level of interest from individuals or institutions that helped finance your small (soon to be bigger) business. Venture capitalists and angel investors usually require an equity share in the firm, so that you surrender some ownership rights. Sometimes they insist on having a say in day-to-day operations, and occasionally even mandate hiring an executive officer of their own choice. Letting go of the steering wheel is not just a trivial adjustment for many entrepreneurs— as we saw in Chapter 5, most entrepreneurs have a strong "locus of control." They think they can control their environment and often need to try to direct their own destiny. Can you let go?

Question 2: By expanding are you diluting beyond recognition the passion that originally started the business?
Entrepreneurs, as we saw in Chapter 5, are usually very creative people who possess a deep and abiding passion for what they do. When the firm expands and the owner comes to rely more and more on others, employees as well as investors, the direction and even the underlying vision of the firm may change. This may be an emotional shock, akin to that of a parent watching a children grow up and leave home. Are you ready to leave some of the creative work to others?

In sum, as Ms. Allon and her co-authors point out, expansion may make you richer but less happy. "Growth and expansion," they warn, "are not always good or desirable." Think carefully about what you really want.

WHEN SHOULD YOU EXPAND?
Let us suppose that, after much thought, you have made up your mind to expand. Timing, as they say, is everything. When should you make your move? The answer to this question has two dimensions, corresponding to the "microeconomic" and "macroeconomic" aspects of the external environment discussed in Chapter 4. The "microeconomic" dimension revolves around conditions specific to your firm and industry, whereas the "macroeconomic" dimension involves an assessment of the state of the entire economy.

Micro Factors Influencing the Timing of Expansion
You should keep your eyes on several key indicators that might suggest the time to expand has come. These "triggers" include the following:

- You are finding it increasingly difficult to satisfy the demands of your costumers.
- Your employees are finding it difficult to complete all of their work may be working overtime.
- Your inventories have been depleted and remain consistently at low levels.
- There has been a distinct change in the economic environment of the industry that clearly heralds greater demand or lower costs. Changes in regulations or changing consumer preferences may reflect this trend.
- A competitor is expanding. It is either making a bid to increase its market share in the existing market, engaging in a form of product differentiation, or diversifying to sell a new product.

The first three of these points are clear signals that you are bumping up against your current productive capacity. They are signals from your customers that you need to grow so that you can continue satisfying their needs. The fourth is a signal that the entire industry may be growing. The fifth is less clear. It is not always true that you should respond in kind to your competitor's initiatives. Maybe your competitor has had a great idea; maybe it has done something stupid. Sometimes the best response to a competitor's bid for market share is to do nothing. Watch closely but think carefully whether to respond and how to respond.

Macro Factors Influencing the Timing of Expansion

Let's assume that the micro conditions in your industry favor expansion. At the same time, you must remain aware that there are more and less propitious *macroeconomic* conditions for moving forward with expansion. Suppose, for example, that the economy is in a recession. GDP is contracting, unemployment is high. Interest rates are low, both because the demand for credit is low and because the Fed is probably keeping them low in an effort to stimulate aggregate expenditures. Times are bad. Perhaps they are so bad, you reason that they have to get better. If the economy is at the bottom of a recession—a "trough" in the business cycle—then paradoxically this may be the best time for you to expand. As the economy grows, you may expect people to start buying more. This is precisely the moment to act in order to increase your productive capacity to meet increased demand in the future. Here is what you should do.

- Interest rates are low, so you should lock into favorable, fixed-rate loans so that you can invest in new capital.
- Wages and salaries are still low, so this is a great time to hire top-notch employees. They are still hungry for jobs, and the cost to you is low.
- Rents and leases are still low. Lock into them now so that you can expand into a new facility while it is still cheap.
- Build up your inventories in anticipation of increased sales.

Of course all of this presupposes that the economy is poised for a recovery. If you are convinced that the economy is in a tailspin and will not recover in the near future then this is exactly the *wrong* time to expand. Remember that timing is everything.

COSTS OF EXPANSION

Expansion inevitably raises costs, so—until revenues catch up—you can expect to take a loss initially. It is essential to anticipate which costs are likely to increase as you grow, and by how much. You also need to cut corners as much as possible (without sacrificing quality, of course), looking for ways to trim costs overall.

Estimating Expansion Costs

Certain categories of costs will grow more than others as you expand. Here are the ones to watch:

Labor

Increasing production will entail an increase in labor costs. Wage and salary costs will obviously rise as you hire more workers. But there are also less obvious costs associated with increasing employment. For one thing, you will incur hiring and training costs. In addition it will take time and effort to "acculturate" new employees to the firm. There will be administrative and personnel management hassles. Do not underestimate these costs of adjustment. Experienced businessmen generally abide by the "25 percent rule," which means new hires do not exceed 25 percent of the existing labor force. Increasing employment by more than 25 percent invariably leads to failure. Don't do too much too fast.

Another thing to consider is that you may become subject to more government regulations as you hire more workers. For example, once you hit a threshold of 25 workers, you become subject to Title VII of the Civil Rights Act. This will put legal constraints on your employment practices and require more paperwork to satisfy federal reporting requirements.

Capital and Equipment

You will need new capital and equipment. Be sure to contact a number of suppliers to compare service and prices. It may be worthwhile to consider leasing equipment. There are two good advantages of leasing:

1. the supplier is responsible for repairs, and
2. the down payment is often low. The disadvantage is that the leasing rate normally exceeds the interest rate you would have to pay to purchase the equipment.

Facility

You may need to build a new store or plant. As with building a house, this is a complicated and costly proposition. Be sure to invite bids from a number of contractors. Check their credentials, reputation, and bonding. Investigate how they work with their subcontractors. Negotiate the building schedule, so that things are done on time. Pre-commit to a payment schedule.

Inventory

You will probably need to increase your **inventory** (the stock of goods you keep in your warehouse ready to sell) in order to satisfy expected future sales. Furthermore, it is normally assumed that the cost of the new inventory will be higher than that of the existing inventory because the latter can be more easily liquidated. You should monitor your inventories carefully. If they are high it could be a sign that demand for your product is very strong or a sign that you are keeping too much inventory and may be able to reduce costs by managing the quantity more efficiently.

How much inventory should you hold? On the one hand, you need more inventory when you expect sales to increase. On the other hand, there are two types of inventory costs to consider. The first is that every time you acquire another unit of inventory there is an **order cost**. This is the amount it costs to write the purchase order, process the receipt, pay the seller, inspect the good on arrival, and so on. Secondly, there are **holding costs** or **carrying costs** of keeping the good in the warehouse. These consist of storage costs, insurance, taxes, and—if you had to borrow to pay for the inventory—interest. You need to weigh the benefits of holding inventory (satisfying your sales) with these costs. This can be quite a complicated problem, but a traditional way of getting a rough idea of the desirable amount of inventory is by using the **Economic Order Quantity (EOQ)** formula:

$$\text{Desired Inventory} = \sqrt{\frac{2 \ \times \ \text{Order Cost} \ \times \ \text{Sales}}{\text{Holding Cost}}}$$

Don't worry about where this formula comes from for now (it is a two-line exercise in calculus that you may have encountered in math classes—yes, calculus is good for something!) Just notice what it tells you: As your sales increase you should plan to increase your inventories, *but by less than proportionately* (because of the square root). Similarly if holding costs increase (perhaps because interest rates are increasing), you should try to reduce your inventories. This suggests that it is precisely at the trough of a recession—when interest rates are low and sales are expected to increase—that you should increase your inventories.

Reducing Costs

You should always to keep your costs down, but it is particularly important to do so as you expand. One very good suggestion for controlling your costs is to keep abreast of the best practices of, and be aware of average costs in, your industry. Read trade publications. There are a number of excellent studies, published annually, that provide data on industry averages and financial statistics. Two examples are Annual Statement Studies (www.rmahq.org/RMA/CreditRisk/ProductsandServices/RMABookstore/StatementStudies/) and the Almanac of Business and Industry Financial Ratios, which can be purchased on Amazon. Studying these statistics may highlight those of your costs that are out of sync with the rest of the industry.

In addition, you should systematically look for cost savings that will lead to the largest reductions on your total costs. To accomplish this, you need to monitor the proportion of total costs associated with each type of cost. Suppose, for example, that wages and salaries constitute 80 percent of your total costs, while office supplies constitute only 2 percent. Let's say that (by haranguing your secretary about saving printer paper) you were able to reduce the cost of office supplies by 1 percent. Your total costs would then fall by 1 percent of 2 percent, or .02 percent. If you find some clever way of reducing labor costs by 1 percent, however, then total costs would fall by 1 percent of 80 percent, or .8 percent. In other words, focus your cost reduction efforts where you will get the most bang for the buck (and leave your secretary in peace).

A catch-all list of other good cost-reducing ideas follows. Note that this is a generic listing that you can pick and choose from and tailor to your specific needs.

- Consider joining a **Group Purchasing Organization (GPO).** A GPO is a group of vendors who join together to have more bargaining power by purchasing inputs in volume. Small food-service providers, for example, can join FoodBuy, a GPO that purchases food from suppliers in bulk.
- Look for synergies with other firms. Consider joint ventures, or share expenses when possible. Our bicycle company, for example, might share the cost of placing an Internet ad with a travel company that is advertising bicycle tours.
- Lease rather than buy equipment. The initial payment may be low, and the provider will be responsible for repairs.
- To reduce training costs look into government programs that subsidize on-the-job training. For example, the Department of Labor offers the Job Training Partnership Act (JTPA) program. The JTPA will pay up to half of a worker's initial salary for up to half a year; it may also help cover training expenses. Most states also provide job-training programs.
- Reduce labor costs by hiring interns, or by compensating sales personnel with commissions rather than salaries.
- As we have emphasized before, you can expect to take losses during the initial phases of the expansion. You should plan to reduce your own executive compensation as manager, at least for a while.
- Look for cheap advertisements. Have your family wear T-shirts with the company logo. Attend trade shows. Submit press releases about your success to the local paper.
- Use the Internet creatively, both for marketing and distributing your product. It is cheap and gives you 24-hour contact with your customers.

FINANCING YOUR EXPANSION

To finance the expansion you have essentially the same options that we discussed in Chapter 6, except that some may be more readily accessible. Let's quickly review the possibilities, and then look more closely at two of them: issuing debt and issuing equity.

Sources of Capital: The Usual Suspects

Here, in a nutshell, are your options.

- You may still be able to get loans and loan guarantees from the Small Business Administration.
- You can borrow, either by taking a loan from a bank or by issuing bonds. Be aware that there has recently been a disturbing growth in "hard money" lenders, who lend cash but require personal property or the business itself as collateral. These are glorified versions of "payday lenders" and should be avoided like the plague. Also be aware that borrowing from the bank will be much easier than when you were starting up because you now have a track record and have demonstrated your solvency. You will also be able to obtain much larger loans than you did as a start-up. Borrowing, however, means paying interest on the debt you have accumulated.
- You can issue stock, or equity. Angel investors or venture capitalists will be much more eager to invest in your firm than before because you have demonstrated your potential for growth. They usually require an equity stake in your firm. Alternatively, you can go public and try to sell shares on the stock market. The advantage of issuing stock is that it offers access to large amounts of capital. The disadvantages are twofold. First, it is costly and complicated to do. Second, it means you have to surrender part of your control of the company to other owners.
- Now that you are well established, there is yet another option. You can finance the expansion from current profits. This is a conservative strategy that may sound hopelessly old-fashioned, but it has three advantages. First, it precludes the need for paying interest associated with debt. Second, it precludes the need to dilute your control of the company associated with equity. Third, it paces your rate of growth to match the growth in demand by your customers. This means you can achieve slow but steady, sustainable, and controllable growth. However, it may not be feasible if you need large, up-front investments; must engage in large advertising campaigns; or must grow very quickly.

Debt, Equity, and Leverage

For simplicity's sake, let's ignore the fifth item on the preceding list, in-house financing. This leaves us with only two broad methods of acquiring capital: debt or equity. It also raises a question that preoccupies Chief Financial Officers (CFOs) and is a central issue in modern financial theory: How much of its investments should a firm finance with debt, and how much should it finance with equity? This is the province of the theory of **capital structure**, and there are entire college courses consecrated to this theory. Here we will just discuss some of the key factors to consider in issuing debt or equity.

Leverage

Leverage (also called **gearing**) refers to any strategy that amplifies changes in the return from an investment. In corporate finance, leverage is the use of debt to multiply the return to equity. Just as you can use a lever to move a large weight using only a little strength, so too can you use debt to induce larger returns to equity.

To see how this works, let's begin with a simple example that will serve as a benchmark. Suppose that you issue $1,000 in equity. You use this money to invest in a project that yields $1,100 in a year. The **rate of return to equity** is the percentage increase in the payoff of the investment relative to the initial amount invested. In this case the rate of return to equity is ($1,100 − $1,000) / $1,000 or 10 percent.

Now suppose that in addition to issuing $1,000 in equity you also issue $2,000 in debt (you sell bonds). Let's say the interest rate on the debt is 5 percent. In a year, you have to pay back the principal of $2,000 plus interest of $100 or .05 × $2,000. Now you have $3,000 to invest, rather than just $1,000. If every dollar invested has a payoff of 10 percent, then in one year you will reap $3,300 = 1.10 × $3,000.

However, you have to pay back $2,100 = 1.5 × $2,000 to your creditors. This leaves you with $1,200 = $3,300 − $2,100 from an initial equity investment of only $1,000. Therefore the rate of return on equity is now ($1,200 − $1,000) / $1,000 or 20 percent. You have *doubled* the rate of return to equity by leveraging the equity stake with $2,000 of debt! Intuitively, borrowing permits you to invest more, so that given the same equity base, the percentage payoff is larger.

This financial alchemy may sound alluring. Why not borrow, borrow, and borrow more? The answer is that leverage is a two-edged sword. *It multiplies gains, but it also multiplies losses.* Suppose, for example, that the economy unexpectedly turns bad, so that the investment loses money by 5 percent: An investment of $1,000 yields only $950 a year hence. If you had issued only $1,000 in equity, its rate of return would be minus 5 percent. If, however, you had issued $1,000 in equity and borrowed $2,000, then your $3,000 investment would have yielded $2,850 in a year and you would still have had to pay $2,100 in interest.

The net payoff, after interest, would be $2,850 – $2,100 = $750 and the rate of return to equity would be ($750 – $1,000) / $1,000 or minus 25 percent. In other words you have leveraged a fivefold increase in your *losses*.

Leverage can be very attractive if you expect to remain profitable in the foreseeable future, or if you expect interest rates to remain low. These were essentially the conditions that prevailed prior to the recent financial crisis. The economy was growing rapidly so profits were increasing; at the same time the Fed consistently kept interest rates low. Many firms were lulled into complacency about their debts and became overleveraged. When the economy tanked their profits fell, and many were forced into bankruptcy. Remember that you still have to pay interest on your debt even if your sales are down.

Benefits and Costs of Debt

Although debt locks you into interest payments, it does not dilute your ownership of the firm. There are two other things to consider in deciding how much debt to issue.

On the one hand, there is a **tax benefit of debt**. As noted in Chapter 2, one of the more perverse aspects of our tax code has been that it imposes double-taxation on corporate profits. Firms pay taxes on their profits directly, through the corporate income tax. If they pay out their profits as dividends, however, then stockholders pay taxes on them again, through the personal income tax. If the firm issues debt then investors pay taxes only on the resulting interest income. What this means is that it cheaper for firms to finance their investments with debt rather than equity.

On the other hand, there is also a **bankruptcy cost of debt**. Firms that issue debt are still liable for their interest payments, even if they are doing poorly. Firms that issue a lot of debt are more likely to default or go bankrupt than firms that rely upon equity. Investors therefore require firms with higher debt-equity ratios to pay higher interest rates to compensate them for the greater risk of bankruptcy. In other words, issuing a lot of debt may entail paying higher interest rates.

The **trade-off theory** of capital structure asserts that the firm should "trade-off" the tax benefits and bankruptcy costs of debt in order to determine the "best" amount of debt. What does this mean in practice for the growing firm? In most cases, the answer seems to be "stability." The conventional wisdom is that the desirable equity position should be between 30 and 50 percent of your total assets (that is, between 50 and 70 percent as debt). As you expand you should try to keep this ratio as stable as possible. Suppose that you become over-leveraged as you expand, so that your equity position drops to, say, 10 percent. Investors may see this as a red flag, signaling a higher risk of default or bankruptcy.

CONCLUSION AND SOME SUGGESTIONS

This chapter examined various factors that should be considered by entrepreneurs who are debating whether to expand, when to expand, how to assess and reduce expansion costs, and how to finance expansion. We conclude with some suggestions about expansion offered by the *Economist Intelligence Unit (EUI)*, a research outfit associated with the news magazine *The Economist*. The EUI report is entitled "Growing Pains: Expansion Strategies for Small Firms" and can be accessed at www.socius1.com/wp-content/uploads/2009/08/expansion_small_firms2.pdf. The suggestions listed here will tie together many of the ideas covered in this chapter and provide concrete advice about expansion. The EUI suggests that managers keep the following rules in mind as their firm grows:

- *Develop a Strategy.* As we have emphasized throughout the last three chapters, it is essential to plan ahead. Think strategically and don't get lost in the minutia of day to day tactics. "At least every month," says the entrepreneur David Bain, "you need to carve out time to think about the strategic positioning of the business." Failure to plan effectively is one of the main reasons firms fail.
- *Find a niche.* Growing businesses need to understand their markets and anticipate the needs of their customers. The best way to do this is to focus on a niche market, because you will know it intimately and there is little danger of competition from other firms.
- *Move quickly.* Opportunities often disappear quickly, but as a small firm you may be able to take advantage of them more quickly than large firms can. FedEx is a great example. The founder of FedEx, Fred Smith, had the inspiration to see that there was a market for overnight delivery of packages. He was able to set up his firm and exploit the opportunity before the (then!) larger shipping firms could respond.
- *Be choosy.* If you are in a service industry like law, engineering, or architecture, it pays to be picky about your clients. Eva Rosenberg, a tax consultant in California, asserts that "by weeding out demanding, lower-paying customers and taking on easier-to-work-with, higher-paying customers, it's possible to be more profitable using the same resources."
- *Watch the books.* For some reason people are more likely to be late in paying small firms than in paying large firms. "My contacts sign the contract, but not the checks," complains Joshua Greenbaum, a consultant in California. Keep your books scrupulously. Having impeccable financial records will make it harder for customers to stiff you.

- *Let clients drive expansion.* If you enter into a new market, you have to spend time and money to establish credibility. It is much better to expand into markets with established customers who trust your reputation. One clever approach is to get customers to commit to the product *before* you launch it. This not only locks in a customer but also serves as an experimental "proof of concept." Mr. Greenbaum says he sometimes even gets clients to pay for pilot projects.
- *Build a growth oriented team.* Make hiring decisions strategically by looking for people who complement your existing skills and who intend to stay with the company for a long time. Avoid hiring people who at first glance seem the best qualified, but who will jump ship when the economy improves.
- *Seek advice.* As we have seen, running a firm is a multifaceted undertaking. It requires knowledge of economics, finance, accounting, marketing, psychology, taxes, and the law. As the firm expands, these issues become more and more complex. Although you should try to absorb as much as possible about anything that impacts your firm, you can't expect to be an expert in everything. Look for experts that you can trust and who have a track record of giving you good advice.

Further Reading

Allon, J., and the editors of *Victoria Magazine. Turn Your Passion Into Profits: How to Start the Business of Your Dreams.* New York: Hearst Books, 2001.

Bovée, C., J. Thrall, and M. Mescon. *Excellence in Business.* 3rd ed. Upper Saddle River, N.J.: Pearson, 2007.

Brickley, J., J. Zimmerman, and C. Smith. *Managerial Economics & Organizational Architecture.* 5th ed. New York: McGraw-Hill/Irwin, 2008.

Economist Intelligence Unit. "Growing Pains: Expansion Strategies for Small Firms." Retrieved July 2010 from www.socius1.com/wp-content/uploads/2009/08/expansion_small_firms2.pdf.

Kinsley, M., and C. Clarke. *Creative Capitalism: A Conversation with Bill Gates, Warren Buffett, and Other Economic Leaders.* New York: Simon & Schuster, 2008.

Meiners, R., A. Ringleb, and F. Edwards. *The Legal Environment of Business.* Mason, Ohio: Southwestern Publishing Company, 2000.

Narayanan, M., and V. Nanda. *Finance for Strategic Decision Making: What Non-financial Managers Need to Know.* New York: John Wiley & Sons, 2008.

Peterson, R. *Principles of Marketing.* Delhi Global Media, 2007.

Small Business Administration. Guaranteed Loan Programs. Retrieved June 2010 from http://www.sba.gov/financialassistance/borrowers/guaranteed/.

Small Business Administration. Small Business Planner, Retrieved June 2010 from http://www.sba.gov/smallbusinessplanner/index.html.

Small Business Administration Office of Advocacy. (2009). Frequently Asked Questions. Retrieved June 2010 from http://web.sba.gov/faqs/faqindex.cfm?areaID=24.

GLOSSARY

accounting profit The residual left after subtracting explicit costs from revenue; called net income by accountants.

acquisition Occurs when one firm purchases another.

advertising The art of persuading people to buy your product.

agency problem (also called the Principal-agent Problem) Arises when one person (the agent) fails to fulfill his responsibilities to another person (the principal) in whose best interests he has a legal obligation to act.

aggregate expenditures The value of all expenditures on domestic goods, which is by definition equal to consumption, plus investment plus government expenditures plus the trade balance.

angel investors Wealthy individuals who finance start-ups.

angel networks (or angel clubs) Groups of angel investors who meet to exchange news about, and coordinate investments in, new firms.

appreciation An increase in the price of a currency.

assets On a balance sheet, things that you own that have value.

balance sheet An accounting statement that constitutes a picture of the financial condition of the firm at a given moment in time.

bankruptcy cost of debt One reason investors require firms with higher debt-equity ratios to pay higher interest rates to compensate them for the greater risk of bankruptcy.

barriers to entry Factors that make it difficult for a firm to enter an industry.

behavioral segmentation Market segmentation based upon observations about how people respond to certain products.

board of directors   A group of people, elected or appointed, who make decisions about corporate governance and help oversee a corporation.

brand loyalty   The tendency of consumers to stay with a particular brand once they have been convinced of its quality.

break-even analysis   A simple method of estimating how much you will have to sell in order to break even.

break-even quantity   The quantity of production at which a firm breaks even.

B2B firm   A business that sells to other businesses ("Business to Business")

B2C firm   A business that sells to consumers ("Business to Consumers").

bubble   A situation in which the price of a financial asset increases simply because speculators expect the price to increase and not because its underlying, intrinsic value has increased.

business cycle   The fluctuations of economic activity during a long-run trend.

business plan   A written report targeted at potential lenders and customers; it succinctly describes what your business is and why and how it will make money.

buyer power   In five-forces analysis, the ability of consumers to negotiate lower prices.

C Corporations   Corporations that are subject to double taxation.

call option   A financial contract that confers the right to buy an asset at a given price, called the "strike price." Call options written on stocks are often used as incentives for managers.

capital   In economics, one of the traditional factors of production consisting of assets that yield ongoing benefits over time. Physical capital constitutes machinery and tools used to produce goods and services; human capital is the stock of skill and knowledge that people acquire through education and experience. See also **financial capital**.

capital gains   The return to a financial asset resulting from an increase in its price.

capital structure   The branch of financial theory dealing with whether and how much firms should finance their assets by issuing debt or equity.

capitalism   An economic system in which the factors of production are owned by the private sector.

cash   Money you set aside in the firm's bank account to sustain operations in the future; see **working capital.**

cash available from savings   Money from your personal savings that can help cover your losses in the start-up.

central bank   The institution responsible for controlling monetary policy. The central bank in the United States is the Federal Reserve, known familiarly as the Fed.

Chief Executive Officer (CEO)   The highest administrative officer of a corporation.

circular flow diagram   A picture depicting how producers and consumers interact with each other in the economy.

closely held corporation   A corporation whose stock is held by a small number of people (often a family) and is not traded.

command economy   An economic system in which the government makes the fundamental economic decisions about what, how, and for whom to produce.

common stock   A form of stock that confers voting rights in a corporation.

competitive advantage   According to Michael Porter, an advantage that a firm possesses over its competitors, allowing it to earn profits higher than the industry average.

concentrated marketing mix   The practice of applying the same marketing methods to reach customers in different target markets.

conglomeration merger   A merger between two firms producing unrelated goods or services.

consolidation   Occurs when a newly created corporation purchases two already existing corporations.

consumer price index (CPI)   A price index that measures the price of a broad bundle of goods that would be consumed by a typical household.

consumption   In macroeconomics, the value of all consumption expenditures by households.

contraction   A phase of the business cycle over which aggregate economic activity is falling.

corporate governance   A system of rules and incentives designed to ensure that the managers of a corporation act in the best interest of its owners.

corporation   One of several forms of the firm, a corporation is perceived and legally treated as a "false person," with full powers to own property, engage in contracts, and in general practice business just like a real person.

cost   That which must be sacrificed in order acquire something else.

cost-plus pricing   A pricing strategy that involves setting price a fixed amount above costs per unit.

creative destruction The hypothesis of Joseph Schumpeter that capitalist economies grow because strong firms flourish while weaker firms are weeded out.

cross-selling Occurs when rising sales of one good stimulate sales of another good.

customer-based segmentation A form of market segmentation practiced by B2B firms, which is based upon the behavioral characteristics of the firms they serve.

data mining The use of large data sets and sophisticated computer and statistical methods to deduce trends in consumer behavior.

debt Borrowing. In corporate finance it usually involves selling bonds, rather than issuing equity, in order to finance investments.

delayed profitability The harsh reality that it takes several years before most new firms start to turn a profit.

demand pricing A pricing strategy that works by extracting some of the value that consumers derive from using the product.

demographic segmentation A form of market segmentation based upon characteristics such gender, race, education, marital status, age, income, and ethnicity.

depreciation In foreign exchange markets, a decrease in the value of a currency; in economics and finance, the decrease in the value of capital over time due to wear and tear.

differentiated marketing mix The practice of using different marketing methods to reach customers in different target markets.

discounted present value (or just a present value) The current value of a series of future payments, given a certain interest rate.

diseconomies of scale Occur when a firm's costs per unit increase as it increases the amount it produces.

distribution A synonym for place, the third of the four Ps of marketing.

diversification The idea that it is possible to reduce risk by "not putting all of your eggs in one basket."

dividends A share of profits that corporations may pay out to shareholders.

double taxation In the United States, most corporate profits are taxed twice, once through the corporate income tax and again when dividends are taxed through the personal income tax.

downsizing Reducing the size of a firm by laying people off.

e-commerce Business conducted online.

Economic Order Quantity (EOQ)   A formula for calculating the optimal amount of inventory.

economic profit   The residual left after subtracting both explicit and implicit costs from revenue.

economic system   The organization of an economy, defining who owns what and who makes what decisions.

economies of scale   Occur when a firm can reduce its costs per unit by increasing the amount it produces.

economies of scope   Occur when it costs less to produce different goods together than it would to produce them separately.

empire building   The hypothesis that managers may be driven to increase the size of theirs firms as a monument to their personal power and influence.

Employer Identification Number (EIN) (or Federal Tax Identification Number)   The number with which the Internal Revenue Service (IRS) recognizes a firm.

entrepreneurship   The act of undertaking innovative activities to produce and sell new products or services.

equity   A synonym for stock.

exchange rate   The price of one currency in terms of another, for example, the number of dollars you need to sacrifice in order to acquire a euro.

expansion   A phase of the business cycle over which aggregate economic activity falls.

expenditures   To accountants, the dollar value of costs incurred in producing a good; called explicit costs by economists. In macroeconomics, expenditures are the total value of purchases of all goods and services by domestic consumers, firms, the government, and foreign countries.

explicit costs   To economists, the actual dollar value of costs incurred in producing a product; called expenditures by accountants.

exports   In macroeconomics, the value of goods that we sell to other countries.

factors of production   The resources used to produce goods and services. The traditional factors of production are land, labor, capital, and sometimes entrepreneurship.

Federal Reserve (or just the Fed)   The central bank in the United States.

financial capital   Money acquired from a lender to finance investments in capital.

firm   The fundamental organizational and decision-making unit of business.

fiscal policy The manipulation of taxes and expenditures by the government to achieve economic, social, or political ends.

five-forces analysis An important method of studying the competitive forces at work in a market; developed by Michael Porter.

fixed costs Costs of producing a good that do not increase with the amount produced.

focus group A small sample of people who are interviewed about their preferences and interests.

form utility The benefit provided by the consumption of a final good or service.

four Ps of marketing The four essential ingredients of a marketing mix: product, price, place, and promotion.

franchise A business in which independent owners adopt the business model and practices of another company. Most fast-food restaurants are franchises.

free rider A member of a team who gets a "free ride" by shirking his own responsibilities and letting others do more of the work.

gearing See **leverage**.

general partnership A **partnership** in which all partners are treated equally by law and are equally liable for debts.

geographical segmentation market Segmentation based upon where people live and work.

globalization The growing interdependence of different countries around the world.

going public Selling **stock** to the public for the first time; see **initial public offering (IPO).**

government expenditures In macroeconomics, the value of all purchases by the government.

Great Depression A period in the 1930s during which most economies in the world suffered a severe and prolonged economic downturn.

Great Inflation A period from the late 1960s until about 1980 during which many countries suffered severe and prolonged inflation.

Great Moderation A period from the early 1980s until the early 2000s during which the economy grew rapidly, there were no serve downturns, and inflation was contained.

Great Recession The severe downturn in aggregate economic activity beginning with the financial crisis of 2008.

group purchasing organization (GPO) An association of vendors who group together to negotiate more favorable costs from large-volume purchases.

holding costs (or carrying costs)   The costs of holding inventory in the warehouse.

horizontal merger   A merger between two firms that provide the same good or service in the same market.

hostile takeover bid   Occurs when the owners of a firm are opposed to a proposed merger with another firm that is attempting to buy it.

hubris   A Greek word meaning "excessive pride." Managers may exhibit hubris by assuming that their great talents will always make a merger or other business decisions profitable.

implicit costs   The cost of producing a good incurred by not using the resource(s) that might have been employed in the next best alternative use, situation, or circumstance.

imports   In macroeconomics, the value of the goods that we purchase from other countries.

income   In accounting, the revenue of a firm; in economics, the payment received by a factor of production for its services (for example, wages and salaries are the income accruing to labor).

incumbent   A firm already operating in a given industry.

inflation   The percentage increase in a price level (like the **CPI**) over time. The presence of inflation means that prices on average are increasing.

inflation rate   The percentage change in a price index over time.

initial public offering (IPO)   The initial sale of stock by a company.

institutional investors   Large organizations, like pension funds, mutual funds, and insurance companies, which invest large amounts of money in the financial markets.

interest   The cost of borrowing money. The interest rate is the percentage extra that has to be repaid in excess of the repayment of the amount borrowed, or principal.

inventory   Goods kept "on the shelf" ready to satisfy future demands.

investment   In macroeconomics, total purchases of new capital equipment by firms plus new residential construction by households plus inventory accumulation by firms.

just-in-time-production   A production method that attempts to reduce inventory costs by producing exactly what is needed when it is needed.

labor   One of the traditional factors of production, it comprises the time and effort people put into producing goods and services. *Unskilled labor* requires no skill; *skilled labor* is the product of training and education.

labor force   Everyone who has a job or who is looking for one.

land One of the traditional factors of production; consists of all non-reproducible natural resources.

learning-by-doing Occurs when workers become more productive the more that they practice their jobs, causing costs to fall.

leverage Any strategy that amplifies changes in the return from an investment. In corporate finance it refers to the use of debt to finance investment; also called gearing.

leveraged buyout Occurs when the purchasing firm in an acquisition acquires the funds for the purchase by issuing debt.

liabilities The value of debts that you owe.

lifestyle companies Small firms owned by people who seek enough income to maintain a certain lifestyle or to achieve financial security for their families, but who have no interest in expansion.

limited liability The legal fact that the owners of corporations are not personally liable if the firm is sued.

limited liability partnership (LLP) A form of partnership that confers limited liability on all partners; often formed by groups of doctors, lawyers, or accountants.

limited partnership A partnership in which some of the partners ("general partners") are responsible for operating the firm, while other partners ("limited partners") receive a share of profits but play no active role in operations and are only liable up to the amount of their investment in the firm.

locus of control A psychological term describing a sense of one's ability to control the external world. It is a trait shared by many entrepreneurs.

macroeconomics The study of the behavior of the aggregate economy.

mainstream niche A niche market that is so broad that it is no longer a niche.

margin of safety The difference between the amount that a firm sells and the break-even quantity.

market An institution that organizes and facilitates the exchange of goods and services.

market economy An economic system in which the private sector makes the fundamental economic decisions about what, how, and for whom to produce.

market extension merger Occurs when a company expands to sell its goods or services in new geographical locations.

market for corporate control   The hypothesis that the threat of hostile take-over bids may solve the agency problem by providing an incentive for managers to work in the interest of owners.

market research   Systematic methods to acquire and interpret data about the demands for goods and services.

market segmentation   The practice of breaking a firm's customers down into distinct target markets.

marketing mix   A strategic choice by a firm of the four crucial elements of a marketing strategy: product, price, place, and promotion. See the **four Ps of marketing**.

marketing strategy   A systematic and comprehensive evaluation of methods used to convince customers to buy a firm's product.

mark-up pricing   A pricing strategy that involves "marking up" (or raising) the price above costs per unit, given knowledge of the demand for the good.

mass production   The production of manufactured goods in large quantities, permitting efficiencies and economies of scale to lower costs.

merger   Occurs when two existing firms agree to join together to create a new firm.

microeconomics   The study of the behavior of individual (or small numbers of) consumers, firms, and markets.

microlending   Small start-up loans supported by the Small Business Administration.

monetary policy   Manipulation of the money supply and interest rates by a central bank in order to influence economic activity.

monopoly   A market in which there is a single seller.

national income   The sum of all income payments to all factors of production. Ignoring a couple of technicalities, national income is identically equal to Gross Domestic Product (GDP).

net income   The residual left after subtracting explicit costs from revenue; called accounting profit by economists.

net worth   The difference between assets and liabilities on a balance sheet.

niche marketing   The marketing technique of serving a narrow group of consumers who share certain attributes.

nominal gross domestic product (GDP)   The dollar value of all final goods and services produced in an economy over a given time period.

normal profit   Occurs when economic profit is zero, so that the entrepreneur is just able to cover both his implicit and explicit costs.

objective approach   A psychological term describing the tendency to be concerned with how another person performs, rather than how that person feels.

ongoing monthly costs   Continuing expenses beginning with the first month of operation; these costs must be distinguished from start-up costs.

option   A financial contract that confers the right to buy or sell something in the future at a price (called the "strike price") agreed upon today. See **call option**.

order cost   The cost of acquiring new inventory.

outsourcing   The practice of employing workers in other countries to provide services previously supplied by domestic workers.

ownership utility   The benefit conferred on a consumer from the smooth exchange of the title to a good.

partnership   A firm owned by more than one individual.

payroll taxes   Taxes that must be paid by the firm on wages and salaries paid to employees; the most common is the Social Security payroll tax.

place   The third of the 4 Ps of marketing; it involves the choice of where a product is sold and how it is distributed to customers. See **distribution**.

place utility   The benefit conferred upon a consumer by selling a good or service at a place that is convenient for that consumer.

post-industrial economy   An economy in which the preponderance of GDP is represented by the production of services rather than industrial goods.

preferred stock   A form of **stock** that does not confer voting rights in a corporation.

present value   See **discounted present value**.

price   The second of the four Ps of marketing; it encompasses not only the price per unit of the good, but also more clever pricing schemes designed to extract revenue from customers.

price discrimination   The practice of charging different prices for the same good to different people or in different markets.

price index   An average of individual prices in the economy.

primary data   Data that you have to collect yourself.

principal   The amount borrowed in a loan.

pro forma income statement   A measure of projected profit or loss over a given time period.

product   The first of the four Ps of marketing; it consists of the product itself as well as other attributes, such as quality and service.

product differentiation   The marketing technique of emphasizing the qualities of a product that make it different and better than those of competitors.

product extension merger   A merger between companies that provide different but related goods or services.

product-use-based segmentation   A form of market segmentation used by B2B firms, which classifies the firms they serve according to the different ways in which they use the product.

profit   The residual left from revenue after paying all costs.

profit margin   Profit expressed as a percentage of revenue.

profit maximization   The principle that firms should act in the interests of their owners by trying to maximize profit; closely related to value maximization.

promotion   The last of the four Ps of marketing; the art of disseminating information about a product and getting customers to buy it.

psychographic segmentation   market segmentation based upon differences in psychological and sociological behavior.

publicly traded corporation   A corporation whose stock is sold and traded publicly.

quick-flip   A start-up designed to be sold to a larger firm in a short time.

rate of return to equity   The percentage increase in the payoff of an investment relative to the initial amount invested.

recession   A period of falling aggregate economic activity.

relationship management   The practice of fostering a long-term relationship with a customer by providing extended service for a product, rather than just selling the product.

rent   Payments for the services of land, or more generally, the payment for any fixed factor of production.

revenue   The dollar value of the sales of a firm; called income by accountants.

risk aversion   The tendency of most people to dislike, and try to avoid or mitigate the effects of, risk.

risk taker   Someone who embraces risk.

rivalry   In five-forces analysis, the struggle of firms for competitive advantage.

S corporations   Corporations that are not subject to the corporate income tax and hence avoid double taxation.

scarcity   The fundamental economic reality that there are not enough resources available to satisfy all wants.

secondary data   Data that has already been collected by someone else.

self-financing   Financing the start-up with your own wealth or assets.

shareholder   A person or corporation who owns stock issued by a firm.

shareholder value   See **value of the firm.**

shareholder wealth maximization   Synonym for **value maximization.**

Small Business Administration (SBA)   A federal government organization that helps small firms.

socialism   An economic system in which the factors of production are owned by the state.

sole proprietorship   A firm owned by a single individual.

specific asset   An asset that can only be used for one particular purpose.

stakeholders   Anyone affected by the behavior of a firm. Examples include shareholders, employees, suppliers, customers, and the community.

stakeholder maximization   The principle that firms should act in the interests of all of their stakeholders, not just their shareholders.

start-up   A newly created firm.

start-up assets   Money, spent in the creation of the firm, which yields *future* benefits.

start-up budget   A budget that specifies expected income and costs of a new firm.

start-up costs   Once-and-for-all expenses that occur before the first month a firm is in business.

start-up expenditures   Money spent in the creation of the firm to acquire *current* goods or services.

start-up financial capital   The amount you need to acquire resources to start your business.

stock   A financial instrument conferring a share of the ownership of a corporation; see **equity.**

stock option   A financial contract that confers the option of buying or selling a stock in the future at a predetermined price, called the "exercise price."

sunk costs   Fixed costs that cannot be recouped.

supernormal profit   Occur when economic profit is positive, so that the entrepreneur is making revenues in excess of the amount required to cover explicit and implicit costs.

supplier power   In five-forces analysis, the ability of suppliers to negotiate higher prices.

switching costs   The costs of leaving one supplier and going to another.

synergies   The benefits accruing from joining forces in a merger or acquisition.

target market   A precisely defined group of customers that a company is trying to serve.

tax benefit of debt   The fact that interest earned on money lent to firms is taxed only once, in the personal income tax, while dividend income is taxed twice, once in the corporate income tax and once in the personal income tax. See **double taxation.**

test market   An experiment that involves selling a good in one place to see how well it does.

threat of substitutes   In five-forces analysis, the ability of consumers to find substitute goods in another market.

time utility   The benefit conferred on a consumer by providing a good or service at a convenient time.

total cost   The sum of fixed and variable costs.

trade balance   In macroeconomics, the difference between exports and imports.

trade-off theory   A fundamental theory of capital structure hypothesizing that firms "trade off" the tax benefits and bankruptcy costs of debt in order to determine the optimal amount of debt.

transactions costs   The costs of making a transaction occur, such as the costs of finding trading partners, communicating with them, writing a contract, paying a lawyer, and so forth.

unemployment   The number of people who want (and are looking for) a job but can't find one.

unemployment rate   The ratio of unemployment to the labor force.

unlimited liability   The legal fact that the owners of sole proprietorships and partnerships can be held personally liable if their firm is sued.

utility   In marketing, the ability of a good or service to answer a consumer's wants or needs.

value maximization   The principle that a firm should try to benefit its shareholders by maximizing the value of its stock; also called shareholder wealth maximization.

value of the firm   The price per share of a firm's stock multiplied by the number of shares. In theory this should equal the value of the dividends paid out by the firm in the future; also known as shareholder value.

variable costs   Costs of producing a good that increase with the amount produced.

variable costs per unit   Variable costs divided by the quantity of the good produced.

variance   An exception to zoning laws granted by a city or municipality to a firm

venture capitalists (VCs)   Companies that pool funds from institutional investors and from rich individual investors to finance promising start-ups.

vertical merger   A merger between a firm and one of its suppliers.

video mining   Watching what customers do in the store on video to observe their behavior and observe how they react to advertising stimuli.

wages   Payment per hour for services of labor. Often used loosely to include salaries as well as hourly wages.

word-of-mouth   The way in which customers spread news about a product (good or bad) by talking amongst themselves.

working capital   A synonym for cash.

year-end balance   The expected difference between costs and income for a start-up; this is the minimum amount of capital that must be acquired from external sources.

BIBLIOGRAPHY

Akerlof, G., and R. Shiller. *Animal Spirits: How Human Psychology Drives the Economy and Why It Matters for the Global Economy.* Princeton, New Jersey: Princeton University Press, 2009.

Allon, J., and the editors of Victoria Magazine. *Turn Your Passion Into Profits: How to Start the Business of Your Dreams.* New York: Hearst books, 2001.

AllTheTests.com (2010). Entrepreneur Quiz. Retrieved July 2010 from http://www.allthetests.com/quiz07/dasquiztd.php3?testid=1076428333.

Baron, J., and J. Hollingshead. "Making Segmentation Work." *Marketing Management.* January/February 2002, 24–28.

Bike Pedlar. Where Was My Bike Made? March 18, 2008. Retrieved June 2010 from http://allanti.com/page.cfm?PageID=328.

Boder, S. *Capitalizing on Change: A Social History of American Business.* Chapel Hill, North Carolina: University of North Carolina Press, 2009.

Bovée, C., J. Thrall, and M. Mescon. *Excellence in Business.* 3rd ed. Upper Saddle River, N.J.: Pearson, 2007.

Brickley, J., J. Zimmerman, and C. Smith. *Managerial Economics & Organizational Architecture.* 5th ed. New York: McGraw-Hill/Irwin, 2008.

BusinessMart, Advantages and Disadvantages of a Start-up Business. Retrieved July 2010 from http://buying.businessmart.com/advantages-disadvantages-of-a-start-up-business.php.

Campbell, J., and R. Shiller. "Valuation Ratios and the Long-Run Stock Market Outlook." *Journal of Portfolio Management* 24 (1998): 11–26.

Carland, J., F. Hoy, W. Boulton, and J. Carland. "Differentiating Entrepreneurs from Small Business Owners: A Conceptualization." *Academy of Management Review 9*, no. 3 (1984): 354–359.

Coase, R. "The Nature of the Firm." *Economica 4* (1937): 386–405.

Economist Intelligence Unit. "Growing Pains: Expansion Strategies for Small Firms." Retrieved July 2010 from www.socius1.com/wp-content/uploads/2009/08/expansion_small_firms2.pdf.

Entrepreneur Centre. "Entrepreneur Training Guide: Catching the Wave." Retrieved July 2010 from http://www.loginstitute.ca/entrepreneur/index.php?id=24&level=4.

Friedman, M. *Capitalism and Freedom*. Chicago: University of Chicago Press, 1962.

———. "The Social Responsibility of Business Is to Increase Its Profits." *New York Times Magazine*, September 13, 1970: SM17.

Glick-Smith, J. "Successful Entrepreneurs." *Intercom* (July/August 1999).

Jensen, M. "Value Maximization, Stakeholder Theory, and the Corporate Objective Function." *European Financial Management 7* (2001): 297–317.0

Jensen, M., and W. Meckling. "Theory of the Firm: Managerial Behavior, Agency Costs and Ownership Structure." *Journal of Financial Economics 3* (1976) :305–360.

Junior Achievement's 2009 Teens and Entrepreneurship Survey. Retrieved July 2010 from http://www.ja.org/files/polls/JA-Teen-Entrepreneurial-Poll-09.pdf.

Kant, I. *Foundations of the Metaphysics of Morals*. (1797). Translated by Mary Gregor. Cambridge: Cambridge University Press, reprinted 1996.

Kinsley, M., and C. Clarke. *Creative Capitalism: A Conversation with Bill Gates, Warren Buffett, and Other Economic Leaders*. New York: Simon & Schuster, 2008.

Kountze, E. "Six Steps to Starting Your Own Business." *Kiplinger* May 21, 2008. Retrieved July 2010 from http://www.kiplinger.com/columns/starting/archive/2006/st0504.htm.

Lowery, Y. Minorities in Business: A Demographic Review of Minority Business Ownership. Small Business Administration Office of Advocacy. 2007. Retrieved June 2010 from http://www.sba.gov/advo/research/rs298tot.pdf.

———. Women in Business: A Demographic Review of Women's Business Ownership. Small Business Administration Office of Advocacy. 2006. Retrieved June 2010 from http://www.sba.gov/advo/research/rs280tot.pdf.

Mankiw, N.G. *Principles of Economics*. 6th ed. Mason, Ohio: Southwestern Publishing Company, 2012.

Marx, K., and F. Engels. *The Communist Manifesto.* 1948. Introduction by Martin Malia. New York: Penguin, reprinted 1998.

McCarthy, C. Facebook Buys Photo Service Divvyshot, cnet news, April 2, 2010. Retrieved June 2010 from http://news.cnet.com/8301-13577_3-20001693-36.html.

Meiners, R., A. Ringleb, and F. Edwards. *The Legal Environment of Business.* Mason, Ohio: Southwestern Publishing Company, 2000.

Missouri Business Development Program. Start-up and Annual Expenses Worksheets. Retrieved July 2010 from http://www.missouribusiness.net/sbtdc/docs/startup_annual_expense.pdf.

Murray, M. Market Segmentation. About.com: Logistics/Supply Chain. Retrieved July 2010 from http://logistics.about.com/od/forsmallbusinesses/a/Market_Segmentation.htm.

Narayanan, M., and V. Nanda. *Finance for Strategic Decision Making: What Non-financial Managers Need to Know.* New York: John Wiley & Sons, 2008.

Peterson, R. *Principles of Marketing.* Delhi Global Media, 2007.

Porter, M. *Competitive Strategy.* New York: Free Press, 1980.

———. "How Competitive Forces Shape Strategy." *Harvard Business Review* March/April, 1979.

Schumpeter, J. *Capitalism, Socialism, and Democracy.* New York: Harper (1942), reprinted 1975.

Simpson, A. Shareholders and Stockholders: The Tyranny of the Or. Asia Corporate Governance Roundtable. 3rd meeting. April 3, 2001.

Small Business Administration. Are You Ready to Start a Business? Retrieved June 2010 from http://www.sba.gov/assessmenttool/index.html.

———. Guaranteed Loan Programs. Retrieved June 2010 from http://www.sba.gov/financialassistance/borrowers/guaranteed/.

———. Small Business Planner, Retrieved June 2010 from http://www.sba.gov/smallbusinessplanner/index.html.

Small Business Administration Office of Advocacy. (2009). Frequently Asked Questions. Retrieved June 2010 from http://web.sba.gov/faqs/faqindex.cfm?areaID=24.

Smith, A. *An Inquiry into the Nature and Causes of the Wealth of Nations.* (1776). Chicago: University of Chicago Press, reprinted 1977.

United States Census Bureau. Annual Survey of Manufactures. Retrieved July 2010 from http://www.census.gov/manufacturing/asm/index.html.

Vidal, D. Reward Trumps Risk: How Business Perspectives in Corporate Citizenship and Sustainability are Changing. *Conference Board Report Q-00216-06-EA. 2006.*

Wolfe, L. Be a Woman Entrepreneur—Start Your Own Business. About.com: Women in Business. Retrieved June 2010 from http://womeninbusiness. about.com/od/startingasmallbusiness/u/startups.htm.

INDEX

Index note: Page numbers followed by *g* indicate glossary entries.